NEW DIRECTIONS FOR ADULT AND CONTINUING EDUCATION

Susan Imel, *Ohio State University*
EDITOR-IN-CHIEF

Women's Career Development Across the Lifespan: Insights and Strategies for Women, Organizations, and Adult Educators

Laura L. Bierema
Michigan State University, East Lansing

EDITOR

Number 80, Winter 1998

JOSSEY-BASS PUBLISHERS
San Francisco

Women's Career Development Across the Lifespan: Insights and
Strategies for Women, Organizations, and Adult Educators
Laura L. Bierema (ed.)
New Directions for Adult and Continuing Education, no. 80
Susan Imel, Editor-in-Chief

Copyright © 1998 by Jossey-Bass Inc., Publishers, 350 Sansome Street,
San Francisco, CA, 94104.

Microfilm copies of issues and articles are available in 16mm and 35mm,
as well as microfiche in 105mm, through University Microfilms Inc., 300
North Zeeb Road, Ann Arbor, Michigan 48106–1346.

ISSN 1052–2891   ISBN 0–7879–1168–2

New Directions for Adult and Continuing Education is part of The
Jossey-Bass Higher and Adult Education Series and is published quarterly
by Jossey-Bass Inc., Publishers, 350 Sansome Street, San Francisco, California 94104–1342. Periodicals postage paid at San Francisco, California,
and at additional mailing offices. Postmaster: Send address changes to
New Directions for Adult and Continuing Education, Jossey-Bass Inc.,
Publishers, 350 Sansome Street, San Francisco, California 94104–1342.

Subscriptions cost $54.00 for individuals and $90.00 for institutions,
agencies, and libraries.

Editorial correspondence should be sent to the Editor-in-Chief,
Susan Imel, ERIC/ACVE, 1900 Kenny Road, Columbus, Ohio
43210–1090. E-mail: imel.1@osu.edu.

Cover photograph by Wernher Krutein/PHOTOVAULT © 1990.

Jossey-Bass Web address: http://www.josseybass.com

Printed in the United States of America on acid-free recycled paper con-
taining 100 percent recovered waste paper, of which at least 20 percent is
postconsumer waste.

CONTENTS

EDITOR'S NOTES   1
Laura L. Bierema

1. Women's Career Development Patterns   5
Pamela J. Schreiber
The author assesses the characteristics and patterns of women's career development and explores alternative work arrangements as options for women
who are striving to balance work and life.

2. Work and Family Issues: Their Impact on Women's   15
Career Development
Rose Mary Wentling
The author explores the challenges of managing work and family and sug-
gests responses that employers can make to ease the tension.

3. Women's Career Development in Midlife and Beyond   25
Vivian W. Mott
The emergence of women working in middle and later life is considered,
with attention to how women's careers in later life present challenges and
opportunities for career development.

4. Women's Career Development at the Glass Ceiling   35
Patricia L. Inman
The author investigates the realities of the glass ceiling and proffers strate-
gies for women whose careers have encountered it.

5. Women's Career Development and Part-Time Arrangements   43
Marcia Brumit Kropf
This chapter discusses the benefits, challenges, and strategies of part-time
work arrangements and explores how part-time employment can be a viable
career development option for women.

6. Human Resource Development's Role in Women's   53
Career Progress
Kimberly S. McDonald, Linda M. Hite
The authors explore the role of human resource development in promoting
the career progress of women.

7. Mentoring and Women's Career Development   63
Catherine A. Hansman
This chapter explores the human resource development strategy of men-
toring and its implications for women's career development.

8. Women's Career Development in Trade Unions: 73
The Need for a Holistic Approach
M. Catherine Lundy
The literature rarely looks at women's development in trade unions. This
author does, addressing the context and process of women's development
in trade unions.

9. Diversity Issues in Women's Career Development   83
Juanita Johnson-Bailey, Elizabeth J. Tisdell
The authors explore diversity in the context of women's career development
through the use of their own personal stories, literature review, and social
critique.

10. A Synthesis of Women's Career Development Issues   95
Laura L. Bierema
This chapter synthesizes the themes, issues, and strategies of this volume.
It assesses the nature of women's career development and recommends
strategies for women, organizations, and adult educators.

INDEX   105

EDITOR'S NOTES

All women work, many of them for pay. Beck (1998) reports that 99 percent of all American women work for pay at some point in their lives. Although women's workforce participation has steadily increased and shows no sign of diminishing, they lag behind men in pay, promotion, benefits, and other economic rewards (Knoke and Ishio, 1998). Despite the progress over the past fifty years, about half of the world's workers are in sex-stereotyped occupations, and women work in a narrower range of occupations than men do. A few women have broken through the proverbial glass ceiling, yet the image of the unshatterable glass ceiling hovers over the careers of many aspiring women. Today roughly 5 to 10 percent of women hold positions of power in organizations, either in executive management or through board membership.

How do women develop in their careers? I was fortunate to have a boss and mentor who charged me with writing a career plan during my first year of a corporate career. At the time, I thought the request was a waste of time and found writing it very difficult. As the years passed and my career progressed, however, I began to appreciate his wisdom. After several years of promotions and career achievement, I became more aware of discrimination and harassment. My career direction changed drastically when I met one of the organization's top executives. When he learned I was working on a doctorate, he asked, "What's it in, home economics?" I was speechless in that moment and troubled for months after. Was this how the company viewed women's development? If he felt that way, were there others? That comment, rude and troubling, was a pivotal moment in my career development. It forced me to take stock of the organization culture and values, and eventually it prompted me to seek a second career.

This volume raises and explores issues unique to the career development of women in the United States. It addresses various aspects of women's career development, along with their implications for women, adult educators, human resource development professionals, and organizations. It articulates the social, political, and economic contexts of women's career development through an exploration of women's career patterns; work and family issues; career development in midlife and beyond; glass ceiling dynamics; women's career development in part-time work; human resource development's role in women's career progress; mentoring; career development in trade unions; and diversity issues. It ends with a synthesis of the issues.

This volume is constructed to illustrate the context, career spans, and issues characterizing women's career development. Although the focus is on women who are in a position to advance in their careers, it should be noted that some women are prevented from ever enjoying career advancement. These women are segregated in low-paying jobs with no mobility whatsoever. Their position is due to educational systems that are unequal based on race, class,

1

and gender; occupational segregation; wage differentials by gender and race; class position of low-paying jobs; and the growth of the contingent workforce (Harlan and Berheide, 1998).

The volume begins with Schreiber's analysis of career development patterns. It notes that the traditional job model of a continuous cycle of employment in one organization is antiquated. The changing nature of work may benefit women who are accustomed to working flexibly with intervals of unemployment (Beck, 1998). The author assesses how women's career development is different from men's, and evaluates the use of alternative work arrangements.

The next two chapters explore issues characterizing the life cycle of women: family and aging. Balancing work and family is a daunting responsibility for career women. Wentling explores the challenges women face while trying to strike this balance and offers strategies for both women and employers to ease the work and family conflict that many women experience. Midlife career development is an emerging issue, especially with the increasing numbers of adults in middle and later life composing the population. Many women elect to work in midlife and beyond for financial reasons, increased longevity, and personal choice. Mott explores the context, attitudes, and challenges associated with career development in these later years.

Chapters Four and Five explore how women have mitigated the glass ceiling and have used part-time employment as strategies for career success. The term *glass ceiling* refers to "invisible, artificial barriers that prevent qualified individuals from advancing within their organization and reaching full potential" (Glass Ceiling Commission, 1998). Inman assesses the issues for career development at the glass ceiling on the eve of a new millennium. Some women choose to work part time as a strategy for balancing work and family. "'Part-time' everywhere still often translates as 'second-class'. That is not to say that there are no good, interesting, secure and well-paid part time jobs around, but just that they are rare. Part-timers are generally regarded as less committed and less valuable than full-timers, and are treated accordingly. One American woman, previously in a high-powered full time job, returned to work part-time after childbirth and found that 'everybody behaved as though I had suddenly gone dumb'" (Beck, 1998, p. 9). Brumit Kropf discusses voluntary part-time arrangements, highlighting the need for such arrangements and the challenges of using them.

The next three chapters focus on human resource development (HRD) strategies for women. They address the response of HRD, consider mentoring, and explore HRD among trade unions. Women's access to HRD programs is an important part of their development. Knoke and Ishio (1998) conducted longitudinal data analysis on a cohort of young workers to document that women's participation in company training programs was at a significantly lower rate than men's. Their study was done to evaluate whether reports of a demise of the gender gap in company training based on incident levels observed in cross-sectional surveys were accurate. Knoke and Ishio's principal conclusion was that the "gender gap in company job training remains far more robust, tenacious, and resistant to explanation than previous researchers had indicated. This discovery admonishes both firms and social researchers to pay more attention to the ways that employees' genders interact with private-sector policies and practices" (1998, p. 153). McDonald and Hite explore HRD's role in women's career progress and evaluate the effectiveness of different approaches. Mentoring, a specific HRD strategy, has important implications for the career success of both women and men. Hansman discusses mentoring and the implications of such relationships for women who are developing in their careers. The focus on HRD initiatives closes with exploring the career development of women in trade unions. Lundy illuminates the career development of women who are members of trade unions, an often ignored population in the career development literature.

The final two chapters put career development into the larger social context. Johnson-Bailey and Tisdell take on diversity from a personal perspective. They offer personal vignettes of their own career development and tie them to the literature. They then move beyond the personal to place career development in the larger social context that is characterized by positionality, unequal distribution of power, segregation, and discrimination. Johnson-Bailey and Tisdell challenge career developers to respond to diversity more proactively. The final chapter, a synthesis of the volume, offers strategies for women, organizations, and adult educators.

This volume strives to illustrate the context, career life cycle, and challenges that characterize women's career development. The career progress of nearly half the workforce can no longer be ignored. It is my hope that this volume will inspire women, organizations, and adult educators to understand the diversity of women's career development and act to continue the work of achieving workplace equality.

Laura L. Bierema
Editor

References

Beck, B. "Women and Work: A Gentle Invasion." *Economist,* Jul. 18, 1998, pp. S6–S9.

Glass Ceiling Commission. U.S. Department of Labor. Washington, D.C., 1998.

Harlan, S. L., and Berheide, C. W. *Barriers to Workplace Advancement Experienced by Women in Low-Paying Occupations.* Washington, D.C.: U.S. Department of Labor, Glass Ceiling Commission (B943073), 1998.

Knoke, D., and Ishio, Y. "The Gender Gap in Company Training." *Work and Occupations,* 1998, 25 (2), 141–167.

LAURA L. BIEREMA is assistant professor in the School of Labor and Industrial Relations, Center for Human Resources Education and Training, Michigan State University, East Lansing, Michigan.

This chapter focuses on the interlocking characteristics of women's career development—the balance of work and family, career interruptions, and diverse career patterns—and explores how alternative work arrangements may offer women options for full participation in the world of work.

Women's Career Development Patterns

Pamela J. Schreiber

Career choice and career development process are different for women because of the social context, which defines certain roles and expectations for them. Although it is certainly more common now than in the past for women to participate in the workforce, their options and opportunities continue to be constrained by traditional views that suggest they are less career oriented and will inevitably face conflict between work and family roles. Once considered abnormal (Super, 1957), women's diverse career development patterns are simply representative of the complex process of managing multiple roles throughout their lifespan. Although research efforts focusing on women's career development have been instrumental in understanding this complex process (Betz and Fitzgerald, 1987), a comprehensive theory has not yet emerged.

This chapter focuses on three interrelated characteristics of women's career development: the balance of work and family, career interruptions, and diverse career patterns. Based in the socialization process for women, this discussion exposes the complex nature of women's career development. Understanding this complexity informs the discussion related to women's participation in alternative work arrangements characteristic of the new world of work, another topic discussed in this chapter. A major point in this discussion focuses on the extent to which these opportunities support women's work lives.

The Distinctiveness of Women's Career Development

Overall, traditional career development theory has been invaluable for supporting development of individuals in organizations. However, several constructs fundamental to these theories are not well suited to women and women's vocational behavior and experiences. One such construct is that of person-environment match, otherwise known as the trait-and-factor perspective (Parsons, 1909). This perspective, foundational to many career development theories, suggests that career choice is a process of matching an individual's abilities and interests with a work experience that requires those abilities and one that satisfies the individual's interests. This person-environment match is completed when the individual becomes aware of his or her interests and abilities, explores options and opportunities in the world of work, and makes a reasonable match between the two. Holland's typology model, one of the most extensively used and researched theories of career choice, is based on this perspective of matching individual interests and traits to a particular work experience (Spokane, 1996).

Although the trait-and-factor perspective is easy to employ and seems to accommodate individuality in career selection, this approach presents some difficulties for women as a group. The socialization process for women is such that females do not have the opportunity to develop any and all interests; often their choices are only those deemed acceptable and appropriate for their gender (Larwood and Gutek, 1987). For example, according to Gottfredson (1996), professions such as librarian, teacher, social worker, secretary and nurse are considered feminine in terms of their sex-type rating. Betz and Fitzgerald (1987) define occupational sex stereotypes as normative views of the appropriateness of various occupations for males and females (p. 31). Women as caregivers and homemakers and men as breadwinners and leaders are stereotypes that dictate the appropriateness of various occupations for females and males.

Women's career choices are made in a context characterized by sex role stereotyping that views their primary role as homemaker separate and somewhat incompatible with career involvement. The majority of traditional career development theories are based on research with men, whose socialization supports career involvement and offers a wide range of options from which to choose. Although not fundamentally different from that of men, women's career development is a great deal more complex because it must deal with a combination of attitudes, role expectations, behaviors, and sanctions known as the socialization process (Fitzgerald and Crites, 1980, p. 45). A useful theory of women's career development must place women's career choices in the context of current social norms and beliefs about women's capabilities and acceptable roles, and must recognize the overt and covert mechanisms that contribute to maintaining these beliefs. Changes in career and life patterns have been slow in coming because gender differences are much more than individuals' attitudes that can be overcome through enlightenment and education. These differences are interwoven into the very fabric of our society (Cook, 1993, p. 228). Throughout the process of selecting a career, a woman will encounter a multitude of issues related to sex role stereotyping, sex discrimination, and multiple role expectations that will significantly affect her choice.

Experiences too shape the development of interests. If females are offered only certain types of experiences or discouraged from pursuing certain other types, the opportunity to identify freely and develop all potential interests is diminished (Nieva and Gutek, 1981). Although matching personal interests to opportunities in the world of work may seem simple, the process of developing interests is quite complex because of the social context. The socialization process for young women sets the stage for work and nonwork role conflict. The fact that women bear children sets up a scenario in which women are considered the primary caregivers and the expectation that their career development must and will be sacrificed in order to fulfill this role. A closer look at work-family balance reveals how women's career development is impacted by these social expectations and the roles they are assigned.

Work-Family Balance. The differences between men's and women's career development begin at the point of career choice. Early research on women's career development posited the work-nonwork (namely family) role interface as an either-or, home-versus-career dilemma. While the focus more recently has been on the *interface* of these two domains, the history of women's traditional roles as homemaker and mother continues to influence virtually every aspect of their career choice and adjustment (Fitzgerald, Fassinger, and Betz, 1995). The extensive research in this area has included comparisons between women with families who work and women with families who do not work, the effect of work on children and on the marriage relationship, and the effect of career interruptions due to family responsibilities on women's career development process.

The world of work has tended not to accommodate combining work and family, the consequences of which have tremendous impact on women (Rosen, 1989). In fact, Betz and Fitzgerald (1987), in summarizing research in this area, concluded that marital and family status has been the most consistent predictor of women's career orientation and innovation. Melamed (1995) measured career success in terms of salary and managerial position using a sample of 457 male and female full-time employees. As hypothesized in this study, marriage and parenthood were negatively related to women's career success. Higgins, Duxbury, and Lee (1994) found that interference from work to family and interference from family to work were greater for women than for men. For men, work and family roles tended to occur sequentially, in that family role responsibilities did not surface until work tasks were completed. For women, these roles occurred simultaneously in that each was permitted to interfere with the other. Although both types of interference decreased somewhat as children entered adolescence, the women in this study spent more time overall than men did on work and family activities, and they experienced higher levels of role overload across the life cycle.

DiBenedetto and Tittle's (1990) study further illustrates the difference between men and women with regard to the work-family role interface. This study found that for men, work-family roles were independent choices; both were available without presenting a conflict. For women, however, these roles were perceived (by both the male and female respondents) as a trade-off situation. In other words, when conflict between the two roles occurred, the women expected to have to make choices between the two domains based on their preferences toward one role or the other. Because women are expected to choose one role over the other and because traditional measures of career success include continuity and total commitment to one's work, women are often viewed as less interested in their career development. The career interruptions that occur when women resolve role conflict by choosing family over work is another characteristic of women's career development.

Career Interruptions. Career interruptions are characteristic of women's career development primarily because of having to choose when combining work and family. While marriage and family have traditionally been viewed as positive for men's careers (representing stability), this combination could reasonably be considered a career liability for women when success is defined by traditional standards (Tharenou, 1995). Felmlee (1995) found an immediate negative effect on women's occupational rewards from only a single break in employment. Schneer and Reitman (1995) found that after controlling for relevant variables, men exceeded women in income and managerial level at mid-career; the researchers attributed these differences to both discrimination and women's early career interruptions. The decision to interrupt employment for family clearly carries significant consequences.

Accommodating career interruptions as a normal and expected aspect of an individual's work life is necessary as workforce demographics change and social values regarding men's roles in the family also change. Fewer than 7 percent of families fit the traditional model, but many workforce policies and practices still view work and family as separate spheres, with husbands and wives in traditional roles (Kerka, 1991). Some companies offer on-site or subsidized child care services, but additional benefits, such as flexible work schedules, flexible benefit packages, alternative work arrangements (such as job sharing and home-based work), and additional legislative policies (such as the 1994 Family and Medical Leave Act), are critical to achieving true work-family balance (Coates, Jarratt, and Mahaffie, 1990; Johnson and Packer, 1987; Watkins, 1988). A career interruption may no longer cost a woman her job, yet it may still cost her in terms of promotions and participation in training and career development activities or in the informal networking that can lead to special projects or strategic (and visible) committee work (Hite and McDonald, 1995).

If successfully balancing work and family roles includes career interruptions, there is great benefit in reconstructing the definition of the successful career path to include interruptions as a normal phase within the career development process (Scheen, 1990, as cited in Swanson, 1992; Schneer and Reitman, 1995). The question of having both family and a career became an issue only after women entered the workforce in substantial numbers; men typically were not asked if they would forgo a family in lieu of pursuing a career or how they planned to manage if they desired both (Baruch, Barnett, and Rivers, 1983). In 1995 24.7 million women in the labor force were parents; 42 percent of these women had children under the age of six (U.S. Bureau of the Census, 1995). Recognizing the need to integrate these two aspects of adult life will lead to a more realistic perspective of successful career development for women and men.

Diverse Career Patterns. The failure of traditional theories to describe and explain adequately the career development process for women is well documented in the literature (Betz and Fitzgerald, 1987; Diamond, 1987; Fitzgerald and Crites, 1980; Stitt-Ghodes, 1997). More specifically, developmental theory suggests a process of achieving certain career development tasks within an age category, and consistent, uninterrupted movement from one career stage to the next. This description, however, is inconsistent with women's experiences (Fitzgerald and Crites, 1980; Kelly, 1991). As early as 1957, Super acknowledged that women's career patterns were different but stated clearly that because of the lack of research on the topic, his book, *The Psychology of Careers,* emphasized only men's career development. The interface between homemaking and working outside the home was the common denominator in the seven classifications of women's career patterns he proposed. In fact, Super stated that a woman's role as child bearer makes her the keystone of the home and therefore gives homemaking a central place in her career. While this statement may be less definitive in terms of women today, the work-home interface remains a key issue in accounting for nonlinear career patterns.

Fortunately, women's career patterns have received increasing attention in the literature since Super's writing, and several more recent studies are worth noting. Young (1992) described the emergence of two themes in her study of women educators. The first theme, *competing urgencies,* described their lives at a time of dual commitment to paid and family work. *Late bloomers,* the label assigned to their career development after their mid-thirties, represented the fact that these women experienced career success through significant accomplishments *after* age thirty-five. None of the women had a definable career plan, and the career themes revealed through this qualitative study represented these women's efforts to find balance and success in their multiple roles.

James (1990) investigated the effect of diverse employment patterns on the psychological well-being of women in midlife. This study found no significant difference in the psychological well-being of women with career patterns categorized as either continuous, interrupted but resumed, or unresumed. Clearly there were consequences for each of the employment patterns considered here, yet the generally high well-being scores suggest that each found her own path to identity resolution. These portraits suggest too that identity concerns are not resolved once and for all, but are often reworked throughout the life cycle. Although the traditional career pattern, represented as linear, planful, and predictable, has been associated with career commitment and success, such studies suggest that career success and fulfillment are clearly obtainable through a variety of career patterns.

Alternative Work Arrangements

Women's career development is characterized by issues related to work-family balance, career interruptions, and diverse career patterns, all intimately associated with their socialization as females in a male-dominated work world. Changes in the world of work, however, are creating an environment in which these issues are becoming as pertinent to men's careers as women's. Alternative work arrangements, such as flexible scheduling, telecommuting, and entrepreneurial opportunities, have emerged in response to advancements in technology and changes in the world of work that demand flexibility, creativity, and maintaining valuable human resources. These alternative work arrangements may finally offer women legitimate opportunities for participating in the world of work in a way that seeks balance among multiple life roles. On the other hand, unless there is a systematic change in the definition of career success with adjustments made in the work environment itself, these options offer no real gain for women or men who view work as only one of many life responsibilities.

Women's past participation in alternative work arrangements has been rooted in the social roles and expectations for their gender. One could say that women have always participated in alternative work arrangements as they have sought creative ways to manage multiple life roles and responsibilities. Unfortunately, women's participation in part-time work, seasonal work, home-based work, or other alternative work arrangements has not historically resulted in overly positive work experiences in terms of satisfaction, salary, promotion, or other employment benefits, such as insurance coverage and paid time off (Amott and Matthaei, 1991; Boris, 1988). Dogged by this history, alternative work arrangements characteristic of the contemporary world of work such as telecommuting, job sharing, and flextime are often viewed with skepticism. These work arrangements have emerged due to changes in the new world of work, but whether they actually offer new, legitimate opportunities for women is hotly debated. Some critics claim that these alternative work arrangements, despite the fact that they reflect the changing world of work, remain exploitive forms of work that simply reinforce stereotypical perspectives about women's participation in the workforce as belonging on the periphery (Haddon and Silverstone, 1993; Phizacklea and Wolkowitz, 1995).

One of these alternative work arrangements, telecommuting, has received sharp criticism as a new form of oppression. Critics claim it is simply a new form of home-based work, a work arrangement that has historically targeted women for low-paying, unstable, unpredictable work (Christensen, 1988; Phizacklea and Wolkowitz, 1995). Even worse, say these critics, work arrangements such as telecommuting from the home (as well as other arrangements intended to accommodate work-nonwork role conflict) strengthen stereotypical perspectives that it is women (not men) who must find creative ways to balance work and family responsibilities. Supporters of telecommuting have suggested, however, that this work arrangement is especially useful for women who, when compared to men, experience more work-nonwork role conflict and more career interruptions, and therefore desire greater flexibility (DiBenedetto and Tittle, 1990; Higgins, Duxbury, and Lee, 1994; Schneer and Reitman, 1995).

In the absence of employee choice and control and an organizational culture of support, alternative work arrangements are no less potentially exploitive. For example, the use of technology does not guarantee any sort of quality for the home-based worker if this work arrangement does not in fact provide flexibility, control, and opportunity. To the extent that alternative work arrangements are considered to lie on the periphery of the world of work, these options will always carry with them career liabilities for those who participate.

The career liabilities most often associated with telecommuting include isolation of the employee from colleagues, supervisors, and others through whom the individual might be exposed to or considered for career development opportunities (Connelly, 1995; Huws, Korte, and Robinson, 1990; Kugelmass, 1995; Nilles, 1994). This out-of-sight, out-of-mind scenario can prove costly for the telecommuter for whom career development is important.

Finally, there is some indication that this work arrangement can be considered only a temporary condition, intended to get an individual through a certain life phase, and may carry negative career development consequences if the worker maintains it for a longer period (Haddon and Silverstone, 1993; Phizacklea and Wolkowitz, 1995). Despite the fact that telecommuting is a relatively new option for participating in the world of work, in reality it may offer women no greater benefits, is no more liberating, or affords no greater flexibility than traditional forms of work.

Conclusion

Adult educators and human resource specialists have many opportunities to contribute during this period of unprecedented change in the world of work. First, additional research in women's career development is necessary. Second, attention must be given to designing alternative work arrangements that offer true options in terms of supporting the multiple roles, responsibilities, and goals for those who participate. Third, new paradigms are needed that assist individuals in understanding their career development in a changing world. Career development strategies that provide opportunities for ongoing career assessment, including personal and professional goal setting, are needed so that individuals can take full advantage of the variety of work arrangements now available.

The world of work is experiencing dramatic changes, and the traditional linear career is becoming less typical for all workers, not just women. Fluidity and flexibility characterize this new world, and the career development process must reflect these characteristics as well (Hall, 1996). Perhaps women's experience with diverse career patterns and balancing multiple role responsibilities will place them in a position to adapt more easily to a world of work where these issues are normal and expected aspects of career development.

References

Amott, T. L., and Matthaei, J. A. (eds.). *Race, Gender and Work: A Multicultural Economic History of Women in the United States.* Boston: South End Press, 1991.

Baruch, G., Barnett, R., and Rivers, C. *Life Prints.* New York: McGraw-Hill, 1983.

Betz, N. E., and Fitzgerald, L. F. *The Career Psychology of Women.* Orlando, Fla.: Academic Press, 1987.

Boris, E. "Homework in the Past, Its Meaning for the Future." In K. E. Christensen (ed.), *The New Era of Home-Based Work: Directions and Policies.* Boulder, Colo.: Westview Press, 1988.

Christensen, K. E. "Introduction: White-Collar Home-Based Work—The Changing U.S. Economy and Family." In K. E. Christensen (ed.), *The New Era of Home-Based Work: Directions and Policies.* Boulder, Colo.: Westview Press, 1988.

Coates, J., Jarratt, J., and Mahaffie, J. *Future Work: Seven Critical Forces Reshaping Work and the Work Force in North America.* San Francisco: Jossey-Bass, 1990.

Connelly, J. "Let's Hear It for the Office." *Fortune,* Mar. 1995, pp. 221–222.

Cook, E. P. "The Gendered Context of Life." *Career Development Quarterly,* 1993, *41* (3), 227–237.

Diamond, E. E. "Theories of Career Development and the Reality of Women at Work." In B. A. Gutek and L. Larwood (eds.), *Women's Career Development.* Thousand Oaks, Calif.: Sage, 1987.

DiBenedetto, B., and Tittle, C. K. "Gender and Adult Roles: Role Commitment of Women and Men in a Job-Family Trade-off Context." *Journal of Counseling Psychology,* 1990, *37,* 41–48.

Felmlee, D. H. "Causes and Consequences of Women's Employment Discontinuity, 1967–1973." *Work and Occupations,* 1995, *22* (2), 167–187.

Fitzgerald, L. F., and Crites, J. "Toward a Career Psychology of Women: What Do We Know? What Do We Need to Know?" *Journal of Counseling Psychology,* 1980, *27,* 44–62.

Fitzgerald, L. F., Fassinger, R. E., and Betz, N. E. "Theoretical Advances in the Study of Women's Career Development." In W. B. Walsh and S. H. Osipow (eds.), *Handbook of Vocational Psychology.* Hillsdale, N.J.: Erlbaum, 1995.

Gottfredson, L. S. "Gottfredson's Theory of Circumscription and Compromise." In D. Brown and L. Brooks (eds.), *Career Choice and Development.* (3rd ed.) San Francisco: Jossey-Bass, 1996.

Haddon, L., and Silverstone, R. *Teleworking in the 1990s: A View from the Home.* SPRU CICT Report Series, no. 10. Brighton: University of Sussex, 1993.

Hall, D. T. *The Career Is Dead—Long Live the Career: A Relational Approach to Careers.* San Francisco: Berrett-Koehler, 1996.

Higgins, C., Duxbury, L., and Lee, C. "Impact of Life-Cycle Stage and Gender on the Ability to Balance Work and Family Responsibilities." *Family Relations,* 1994, *43,* 144–150.

Hite, L. M., and McDonald, K. S. "Gender Issues in Management Development: Implications and Research Agenda." *Journal of Management Development,* 1995, *11* (4), 5–15.

Huws, U., Korte, W. B., and Robinson S. *Telework: Towards the Elusive Office.* New York: Wiley, 1990.

James, J. J. "Women's Employment Patterns and Midlife Well-Being." In H. Y. Grossman and N. L. Chester (eds.), *The Experience and Meaning of Work in Women's Lives.* Hillsdale, N.J.: Erlbaum, 1990.

Johnson, W. B., and Packer, A. *Workforce 2000: Work and Workers for the Twenty-First Century.* Indianapolis: Hudson Institute, 1987. (ED 290 887)

Kelly, R. *The Gendered Economy: Work, Career, and Success.* Thousand Oaks, Calif.: Sage, 1991.

Kerka, S. *Balancing Work and Family.* Columbus, Ohio: ERIC Clearinghouse on Adult, Career, and Vocational Education, 1991. (ED 329 810)

Kugelmass, J. *Telecommuting: A Manager's Guide to Flexible Work Arrangements.* San Francisco: New Lexington Books, 1995.

Larwood, L., and Gutek, B. A. "Working Toward a Theory of Women's Career Development." In B. A. Gutek and L. Larwood (eds.), *Women's Career Development*. Thousand Oaks, Calif.: Sage, 1987.

Melamed, T. "Career Success: The Moderating Effect of Gender." *Journal of Vocational Behavior*, 1995, *47*, 35–60.

Nieva, V. F., and Gutek, B. A. *Women and Work: A Psychological Perspective*. New York: Praeger, 1981.

Nilles, J. M. *Making Telecommuting Happen: A Guide for Telemanagers and Telecommuters*. New York: Van Nostrand Reinhold, 1994.

Parsons, F. *Choosing a Vocation*. Boston: Houghton Mifflin, 1909.

Phizacklea, A., and Wolkowitz, C. *Homeworking Women: Gender, Racism and Class at Work*. Thousand Oaks, Calif.: Sage, 1995.

Rosen, O. C. *Women, Work and Achievement: The Endless Revolution*. New York: St. Martin's Press, 1989.

Schneer, J. A., and Reitman, F. "The Impact of Gender as Managerial Careers Unfold." *Journal of Vocational Behavior*, 1995, *47* (3), 290–315.

Spokane, A. R. "Holland's Theory." In D. Brown and L. Brooks (eds.), *Career Choice and Development*. San Francisco: Jossey-Bass, 1996.

Stitt-Ghodes, W. L. *Career Development: Issues of Gender, Race and Class*. Information Series no. 371. Columbus: Ohio State University, College of Education, 1997.

Super, D. *The Psychology of Careers*. New York: HarperCollins, 1957.

Swanson, J. L. "Vocational Behavior, 1989–1991: Life-Span Career Development and Reciprocal Interaction of Work and Nonwork." *Journal of Vocational Behavior*, 1992, *41*, 101–161.

Tharenou, P. "Correlates of Women's Chief Executive Status: Comparisons with Men Chief Executives and Women Top Managers." *Journal of Career Development*, 1995, *21* (3), 201–212.

U.S. Bureau of the Census. *Statistical Abstract of the United States*. (115th ed.). Washington, D.C.: U.S. Government Printing Office, 1995.

Watkins, K. "Supporting Women's Reentry to the Workplace." In L. H. Lewis (ed.), *Addressing the Needs of Returning Women*. New Directions for Continuing Education, no 39. San Francisco: Jossey-Bass, 1988.

Young, B. "On Careers: Themes from the Lives of Four Western Canadian Women Educators." *Canadian Journal of Education*, 1992, *17* (2), 148–161.

PAMELA J. SCHREIBER *is associate director of university housing and a doctoral candidate in the Department of Adult Education, University of Georgia, Athens, Georgia.*

Employer support programs can help women manage work and family issues.

Work and Family Issues: Their Impact on Women's Career Development

Rose Mary Wentling

Understanding the interaction of work and family issues has become important with the increasing numbers of women in the workforce (Bailyn, 1992; Farber, 1996; Parasuraman and Greenhaus, 1997). According to the U.S. Bureau of Labor Statistics (1998), 76 percent of married women with children ages six to seventeen years old are in the labor force, and 64 percent of women with children under age six work outside the home. In 1997 approximately 60 percent of American women were in the labor force, up from 33 percent in 1950. Women now represent 46.2 percent of the workforce, up from 29 percent in 1950, and they will comprise approximately 48 percent of the workforce by 2005 (Bureau of Labor Statistics, 1998).

Increasingly men are neither the sole nor the primary source of family income. In 1993 women were the sole earners in 20 percent of American married-coupled families, up from 14 percent in 1980. Currently 60 percent of employed men are married to employed wives. Further, women are the sole earners in nearly two-thirds of families maintained by a single person, a category that increased from 12 percent 1980 to 16 percent in 1993 (Judy and D'Amico, 1997).

Postsecondary educational attainment among women has been climbing since the 1960s. In 1994 women outnumbered men among the recipients of postsecondary degrees at every level except doctoral. Women now account for 55 percent of bachelor's degrees, 53 percent of master's degrees, and nearly 40 percent of doctorates. Historically educational attainment has been a predictor of increased labor force participation (National Center for Education Statistics, 1997; U.S. Department of Labor, 1994).

Women are expected to fill 57 percent of the projected 25 million new jobs between 1990 and 2005. This influx of women into the workforce may be the most significant change in the history of the American workplace (Judy and D'Amico, 1997; U.S. Department of Labor, 1994) and will greatly affect work and family issues.

An Overview of Work and Family

Most families in the United States have women and men breadwinners, and most children have working parents (Ford Foundation, 1989). Today only 10 percent of American families fit the traditional model of a two-parent family with children, a wage-earning husband, and a homemaker wife. Workforce demographic changes are evident among women workers who are wives and mothers from married-couple families, never-married mothers, single parents, and divorced, separated, or widowed women.

The reasons mothers work were highlighted in a study prepared for the Joint Economic Committee of the U.S. Congress in 1986. According to the report 71 percent of mothers who work do so "to support their families," not "for something interesting to do" or "to earn extra money." Among the other reasons are economic necessity, increased education, the high cost of living, a desire for personal fulfillment, and the high rate of divorce (U.S. Department of Labor, 1994). According to Parasuraman and Greenhaus (1997), "Business, industry, and the economy as a whole would collapse if women with children were to withdraw from the workforce" (p. 5). As women assume work and family responsibilities, conflict is likely to emerge.

Work and Family Conflict

Work and family conflict arises when work role demands are incompatible with family role demands (Adams, King, and King, 1996; Parasuraman and Greenhaus, 1997). Work and family conflict can occur when the employee: works long hours; has a burdensome work schedule involving overtime, weekend work, travel demands, or shift work; has little control over the hours worked; has a job with little autonomy; is very absorbed in the job; has no job security; has changed jobs due to promotion, layoff, or relocation; has a physically or mentally demanding job; has a negative social climate at work; has unsupportive coworkers; has an insensitive supervisor; and works for a company with inflexible work policies (Friedman, 1991). Conflict increases the possibility that employees will work less efficiently.

Friedman (1991) suggests that relationships, family structure, and the support services available have a bearing on work and family conflict. From a review of over eighty studies of work and family issued between 1985 and 1990, she found that families contribute to work and family conflict when the employee has: a disapproving spouse; inequities in the marriage; an unequal division of home labor; children, especially preschoolers; unstable child care arrangements; and elder care responsibilities, especially when relatives live at a distance.

The level and nature of work and family conflict vary for men and women, and for workers within different income groups and job categories (Friedman, 1991). However, stress, pregnancy, child care, and elder care seem to create the most extensive problems (Friedman, 1991; Neal, Chapman, Ingersoll-Dayton, and Emlen, 1993; Roskies and Carrier, 1994; Thomas and Ganster, 1995).

Stress. The potential for stress increases as workers struggle to balance work and family responsibilities. Stress is a growing health issue in business, leading to poor job performance, absenteeism, and a variety of health problems. The American Medical Association estimates that over 80 percent of medical problems are stress related (Friedman, 1991). These numbers lead some observers to estimate the toll of stress on society at $150 billion, and they regard it as one of the most pressing issues of our time (Friedman, 1991; Trocki and Orioli, 1994).

Pregnancy. Pregnancy and childbirth can create problems for women workers. Prenatal care is expensive and may require time away from work. Most pregnant women experience periods of fatigue or sickness that affect their work performance. All must stop work, even for a few days, for delivery and recuperation. Childbirth and neonatal care are expensive, and worry about finding suitable infant care or returning to work sooner than they are ready can have a negative impact on women's work performance (Friedman, 1991; Waldfogel, 1997).

Child Care. The quantity and quality of affordable child care causes women to miss work or feel stressed about their children's welfare. Scharlach (1995) shows that despite backup arrangements, nearly one-third of parents reported child care breakdowns over a three-month period. The study also reports that employed mothers miss an average of four days a year to manage child-related concerns, such as illness. A child care shortage may result in a provider selection that is unsatisfactory or too expensive, adding emotional or financial strain. These daily strains coupled with the emergencies created by sick children, sick providers, or child care breakdowns lead to employee absences (Friedman, 1991; U.S. Department of Labor, 1994).

Elder Care. An estimated 15 percent of adults bear responsibilities for the care of aging parents or other elderly relatives (Friedman and Galinsky, 1992). Aging issues will escalate in the next century with people living longer and composing a larger share of the population. As the baby boomers (individuals born between 1946 and 1964) age, 19 million people will become dependent on their relatives for care by the year 2040 (Creedon, 1986; Friedman, 1991). According to Friedman (1991), more employees will have dependent elders in the next century than dependent children. Employees may also have more parents (including in-laws) than children. Employees with elder care responsibilities experience high stress levels, absenteeism, and lateness. Effects on work performance are attributed to the stress associated with combining work and caregiving (Friedman, 1991; Ford Foundation, 1989).

Challenges for Women in Managing Work and Family Issues

Every study on the division of household tasks has found that women continue to perform far more chores than men do. This holds true regardless of whether the wife works outside the home full time, part time, or not at all (Ford Foundation, 1989; Neal, Chapman, Ingersoll-Dayton, and Emlen, 1993; Powell, 1997). The findings of the National Study of the Changing Workforce by the Families and Work Institute revealed that 40 to 50 percent of employed women experience conflict, guilt, and stress about their dual roles (Galinsky, Bond and Friedman, 1993). A survey of working adults conducted by the *New York Times* reports that 83 percent of working mothers experience conflict between work demands and the desire to be with family (Galinsky, Johnson and Friedman, 1993). Further, nearly 40 percent of women surveyed reported that their job interferes with family life. Over 30 percent of women have tried to cope with this stress by declining a new job, promotion, or transfer because it would have meant less family time (Galinsky, Johnson and Friedman, 1993).

Constant interference of family with work responsibilities can hinder women's career progression, decrease satisfaction with work, interfere with concentration on the job, increase absenteeism, and perhaps eventually lead to turnover (Parasuraman and Greenhaus, 1997).

Easing Work and Family Conflict

Many employers are customizing benefits to meet new American work and family patterns. Studies have found that employees in more supportive work environments have less work and family conflict and are more satisfied and committed workers (Adams, King, and King, 1996; Galinsky, Bond, and Friedman, 1993; Glass and Estes, 1997). This section focuses on three kinds of employer support identified in the work and family literature: policies, benefits, and services (Auerbach, 1990; Creedon and Tiven, 1989; Neal, Chapman, Ingersoll-Dayton, and Emlen, 1993; Scharlach, Lowe, and Schneider, 1991).

Policies. Policies, both formal and informal, set the parameters for the structure of work. Research shows that a flexible work structure, including the number of hours worked and how work is scheduled, is one of the most important types of support that employers can provide for employees with family responsibilities (Christensen and Staines, 1990; Neal, Chapman, Ingersoll-Dayton, and Emlen, 1993). Employers that seek to increase work flexibility can reduce the number of hours worked (such as part-time work, job sharing, voluntary reduced time, family and sick leave), change where work is done (such as telecommuting and off-site work), and initiate alternative work schedules over a day, week, month, or year (through a compressed work week and flextime) (Christensen and Staines, 1990; Neal, Chapman, Ingersoll-Dayton, and Emlen, 1993).

Working part time can be particularly useful to women with newborn or newly adopted children and those with elder care responsibilities (Neal, Chapman, Ingersoll-Dayton, and Emlen, 1993). In addition, women who can choose part-time work are able to stay in the workforce when family responsibilities prevent their working full time, and they can continue to maintain their skills, and supplement their income (U.S. Department of Labor, 1994).

Among the options that reduce number of hours worked are leave policies—for example, paid or unpaid sick leave, family illness days or hours, personal leave, and family leave (Neal, Chapman, Ingersoll-Dayton, and Emlen, 1993). This option is especially useful for women who must sometimes take time off for medical reasons to care for ill family members, attend to personal needs, or prepare for the birth or adoption of a child (Bureau of National Affairs, 1988). Prior to 1993, there was no federal legislation requiring U.S. employers to offer parental leave, and only a few states had mandated job protection. This changed with the passage of the Family and Medical Leave Act (FMLA), which now requires medium-sized and large companies to supply twelve weeks of unpaid leave annually for the birth or adoption of a child, illness of the employee, or illness of a family member. Although the leave is for a comparatively short duration and is unpaid, it represents an important change in U.S. company policy (Ruhm and Teague, 1997; U.S. Department of Labor, 1994).

Benefits. Most employees are eligible for a set of benefits that their employer chooses to offer, in addition to those benefits that are required legally. There are two basic types of benefits plans that employers usually offer to their employees: an identical set of benefits for all employees in a specific company and the flexible (or "cafeteria") approach, in which employees choose among two or more benefits with respect to all or part of the employer's contributions for employees' benefits (Friedman and Johnson, 1997; Neal, Chapman, Ingersoll-Dayton, and Emlen, 1993).

Flexible benefits plans are more relevant for employees with family responsibilities because they give employees choices from a menu of benefits or cash compensation (Canan and Mitchell, 1991). Such plans recognize that individual employees' benefits needs differ depending on the employee's age, salary, and family status, which helps women customize benefits according to family needs (Canan and Mitchell, 1991; U.S. Department of Labor, 1994).

Services. Employer-supported services addressing employees' family responsibilities can be organized into four categories with varying levels of employer involvement and investment: education, information and referral, counseling and support, and direct services for care recipients (Bureau of National Affairs, 1988; Neal, Chapman, Ingersoll-Dayton, and Emlen, 1993).

Some companies use educational methods, such as corporate libraries, newsletters, guidebooks, and seminars, to provide employees information on a variety of topics, such as parenting skills, how to choose child care services, elder caregiving and other services, prenatal health, latchkey kids, and family relationships. The advantages of these educational resources are that they save women employees time and energy (Bureau of National Affairs, 1988; Scharlach, Lowe, and Schneider, 1991).

Company-based information and referral programs are intended to inform employed caregivers about services available to them and their dependents and help them locate these services. Companies that provide information and referral generally focus on helping employees find child care or elder care arrangements. The advantages of the information and referral services for women employees are the same as those for education.

Some companies provide assistance to employees who are coping with work and family problems—for example, professional counseling, support groups, and peer support. Among some of the difficulties addressed by counseling and support programs are "emotional, marital and family problems, and problems connected with children and aging" (Bureau of National Affairs, 1988, p. 22). Counseling and support services for women employees provide the same benefits as for education and information and referral. In addition, women employees may feel less emotionally drained and more able to concentrate on their work activities after participating in counseling and support programs (Neal, Chapman, Ingersoll-Dayton, and Emlen, 1993).

Increasingly companies are assisting employees with their family dependent care needs directly by providing subsidies, vouchers, or discounts for particular services (Friedman and Johnson, 1997; Neal, Chapman, Ingersoll-Dayton, and Emlen, 1993). Some of these programs may include on-site and near-site child care centers, day care consortiums, child care voucher systems, sick and emergency day care, after-school and summer arrangements, and day care for the elderly (Friedman and Johnson, 1997). Women employees who have access to these programs experience less of the stress resulting from lack of quality and affordable child and elderly care. Further, these programs may enable women employees to spend more time with their children, especially if the company offers on-site or near-site child care centers (Bureau of National Affairs, 1988).

Implications for Women's Career Development

Many of the benefits noted are geared at freeing time for women to attend to family needs. Yet as long as organizations continue to reward the full commitment of employees, flexibility, even when available, will be seen as a liability for career development for women (Brett, 1997).

Although the traditional option of men as breadwinners and women as caretakers is no longer viable economically or psychologically, women are still expected to be primarily responsible for family matters. Therefore, options such as part-time work, flextime, and job sharing are more likely to be used by women than by men. This difference is likely to increase the disadvantages that women already face in the workplace, such as the wage gap, poverty, and the glass ceiling (Bailyn, 1992; Glass and Estes, 1997).

One of the most important conclusions of research comparing men and women is that work and family conflict is not a gender issue. Rather, it is related to family roles and responsibilities traditionally based on gender (Crouter, 1984). Bergmann (1997) suggests that a major reason that "husbands of employed women continue to withhold their labor from the task of running the household has been the strength and persistence of the ideology that declares each task as appropriate for a person of a particular sex" (p. 277).

Hart (1995) argues that children should be considered an issue of general concern rather than solely a women's issue. She asks, "Why should it be a woman's issue to raise the next generation of workers and citizens?" and then reframes the family issue of parenting as "living and working with children," making it everyone's issue. By looking at parenting as a central focus for any educational thought and action concerning work, work and family issues would no longer be separated. Instead they would be intertwined in the adult learning process and workplace.

Organizations must not view balancing work and family as a woman's issue, but rather as a human issue. As long as work and family conflict is seen as a woman's issue, organizations' work and family efforts will not become part of the workplace culture (Greenhaus and Parasuraman, 1997; Powell, 1997). Altering the culture of the workplace with respect to gender roles will require addressing more general societal attitudes, such as the pervasive belief that women should be primarily responsible for the home.

Supervisors and managers must support the process of designing and implementing family-supportive policies and benefits (Raabe and Gessner, 1988; Scharlach, Lowe, and Schneider, 1991). They must thus understand the value of the family life experience in maintaining the stability and effectiveness of the organization (Christensen, 1997). The Bank Street College and Family Life Studies, which examined job and family demands of parents in several companies, found that supervisors and managers play a key role, especially for men (Bailyn, 1992). A father who assumes responsibility for family matters is taking up a nontraditional role and is far more sensitive to his employer's response. Until the workplace sets a higher value on the needs of family, women and men will feel constrained and stressed when taking up a more active family role.

Women's successful career development will involve linking family needs to career decisions, so that work and family roles are in balance. Women face critical decisions around establishing equitable divisions of labor at home. If women today and in the future are to balance work and family responsibilities more effectively, solutions must respect the complexity of the relationship between work and family and consider the sources of conflict. Research and company experience reveal that effective solutions call for fundamental changes in how employees are valued, respected, assessed, managed, trained, and promoted (Friedman and Johnson, 1997; Hammonds, 1997). The focus must be understanding the factors in the work environment, cultural norms, managerial practices, and work processes that are the strongest predictors of work and family conflict and stress, as well as the negative work behavior results (Friedman and Johnson, 1997).

Organizations need to recognize that work and family issues involve work as much as family, and many of the root causes of work and family stress stem from the way organizations and work are structured. Since the resolution of employees' work and family dilemmas can improve the long-term effectiveness of the organization, corporate initiatives must not be seen as benefits or accommodations for women, but rather as management strategies to attain business objectives (Greenhaus and Parasuraman, 1997).

Conclusion

To remain globally competitive, American companies must fully use the talent of both their male and female employees. Companies will no longer be able to rely on procedures designed for a more homogeneous workforce where 100 percent commitment to work and organization is presumed. Instead a system that provides fairness to both men and women will be necessary (Bailyn, 1992). As diversity in the U.S. workforce becomes a key issue, organizations must understand that different people see things differently, respond differently to procedures, behave in different ways, and have different needs. Organizations will need to question the ways things have always been done and improve their organizational processes in addressing work and family issues (Bailyn, 1997). It is more important than ever before for business leaders to align work and family issues with the corporate culture and consider them in their strategic planning. As companies deal with the changes brought on by globalization and technology, they must use work and family concerns as levers for change (Friedman and Johnson, 1997). This task may not be easy, but it will be necessary if organizations are to compete in a diverse and rapidly changing world and at the same time allow their employees to deal more easily with family concerns. Only by such efforts will it be possible to integrate U.S. companies' work-related productivity needs with the family issues that now confront the U.S. workforce.

References

Adams, G. A., King, L. A., and King, D. W. "Relationships of Job and Family Involvement, Family Social Support, and Work-Family Conflict with Job and Life Satisfaction." *Journal of Applied Psychology*, 1996, *81* (4), 411–420.

Auerbach, J. D. "Employer-Supported Child Care as a Women-Responsive Policy." *Journal of Family Issues*, 1990, *11* (3), 384–400.

Bailyn, L. "Changing the Conditions of Work: Implications for Career Development." In D. H. Montross and C. J. Shinkman (eds.), *Career Development: Theory and Practice.* Springfield, Ill.: Thomas, 1992.

Bailyn, L. "The Impact of Corporate Culture on Work-Family Integration." In S. Parasuraman and J. H. Greenhaus (eds.), *Integrating Work and Family: Challenges and Choices for a Changing World.* Westport, Conn.: Quorum, 1997.

Bergmann, B. R. "Work-Family Policies and Equality Between Women and Men." In F. D. Blau and R. G. Ehrenberg (eds.), *Gender and Family Issues in the Workplace.* New York: Russell Sage Foundation, 1997.

Brett, J. M. "Family, Sex, and Career Advancement." In S. Parasuraman and J. H. Greenhaus (eds.), *Integrating Work and Family: Challenges and Choices for a Changing World.* Westport, Conn.: Quorum Books, 1997.

Bureau of National Affairs. *33 Ways to Ease Work/Family Tensions—An Employer's Checklist.* Rockville, Md.: Buraff, 1988.

Canan, M. J., and Mitchell, W. D. *Employee Fringe and Welfare Benefits Plans.* St. Paul, Minn.: West, 1991.

Christensen, K. E., and Staines, G. L. "Flextime: A Viable Solution to Work/Family Conflict?" *Journal of Family Issues,* 1990, *11* (4), 455–476.

Christensen, P. M. "Toward a Comprehensive Work/Life Strategy." In S. Parasuraman and J. H. Greenhaus (eds.), *Integrating Work and Family: Challenges and Choices for a Changing World.* Westport, Conn.: Quorum, 1997.

Creedon, M. *Issues for an Aging America: Employees and Elder Care.* Bridgeport, Conn.: Center for the Study of Aging, 1986.

Creedon, M., and Tiven, M. *Eldercare in the Workplace.* Washington, D.C.: National Council on the Aging, 1989.

Crouter, A. C. "Spillover from Family to Work: The Neglected Side of the Work-Family Interface." *Human Relations,* 1984, 37 (6), 435–447.

Farber, R. S. "An Integrated Perspective on Women's Career Development Within a Family." *American Journal of Family Therapy,* 1996, 24 (4), 329–342.

Ford Foundation. *Work and Family Responsibilities: Achieving a Balance.* New York: Ford Foundation, 1989.

Friedman, D. E. *Linking Work-Family Issues to the Bottom Line.* New York: Conference Board, 1991.

Friedman, D. E., and Galinsky, E. "Work and Family Issues: A Legitimate Business Concern." In S. Zedeck (ed.), *Work, Families, and Organizations.* San Francisco: Jossey-Bass, 1992.

Friedman, D. E., and Johnson, A. A. "Moving from Programs to Culture Change: The Next Stage for the Corporate Work-Family Agenda." In S. Parasuraman and J. H. Greenhaus (eds.), *Integrating Work and Family: Challenges and Choices for a Changing World.* Westport, Conn.: Quorum, 1997.

Galinsky, E., Bond, J. T., and Friedman, D. E. *The Changing Workforce: Highlights of the National Study.* New York: Families and Work Institute, 1993.

Galinsky, E., Johnson, A. A., Friedman, D. E. *The Work-Life Business Case: An Outline of a Work in Progress.* New York: Families and Work Institute, 1993.

Glass, J. L., and Estes, S. B. "The Family Responsive Workplace." *Annual Review of Sociology,* 1997, 23 (5), 289–302.

Greenhaus, J. H., and Parasuraman, S. "The Integration of Work and Family Life: Barriers and Solutions." In S. Parasuraman, and J. H. Greenhaus (eds.), *Integrating Work and Family: Challenges and Choices for a Changing World.* Westport, Conn.: Quorum, 1997.

Hammonds, K. H. "Work and Family." *Business Week,* Sept. 15, 1997, pp. 96–99.

Hart, M. "Motherwork: A Radical Proposal to Rethink Work and Education." In M. Welton (ed.), In *Defense of the Lifeworld: Critical Perspectives on Adult Learning.* New York: State University of New York Press, 1995.

Judy, R. W., and D'Amico, C. D. *Workforce 2020: Work and Workers in the 21st Century.* Indianapolis, Ind.: Hudson Institute, 1997.

National Center for Education Statistics. *Digest of Education Statistics.* Washington, D.C.: U.S. Government Printing Office, Dec. 1997.

Neal, M. B., Chapman, N. J., Ingersoll-Dayton, B., and Emlen, A. C. *Balancing Work and Caregiving for Children, Adults, and Elders.* Thousand Oaks, Calif.: Sage, 1993.

Parasuraman, S., and Greenhaus, J. H. "The Changing World of Work and Family." In S. Parasuraman and J. H. Greenhaus (eds.), *Integrating Work and Family: Challenges and Choices for a Changing World.* Westport, Conn.: Quorum, 1997.

Powell, G. N. "The Sex Difference in Employee Inclinations Regarding Work-Family Programs: Why Does It Exist, Should We Care, and What Should Be Done About It (If Any-
thing)?" In S. Parasuraman and J. H. Greenhaus (eds.), *Integrating Work and Family:
Challenges and Choices for a Changing World.* Westport, Conn.: Quorum, 1997.

Raabe, P. H., and Gessner, J. C. "Employer Family-Supportive Policies: Diverse Variations
on the Theme." *Family Relations,* 1988, 37 (4), 196–202.

Roskies, E., and Carrier, S. "Marriage and Children for Professional Women: Asset or Liability?" In G. Keita and J. Hurrell, Jr. (eds.), *Job Stress in a Changing Workforce: Investigating Gender, Diversity, and Family Issues.* Washington, D.C.: American Psychology
Association, 1994.

Ruhm, C. J., and Teague, J. L. "Parental Leave Policies in Europe and North America." In
F. D. Blau and R. G. Ehrenberg (eds.), *Gender and Family Issues in the Workplace.* New
York: Russell Sage Foundation, 1997.

Scharlach, A. E. *The Family Medical and Leave Act of 1993: Analysis and Appraisal.* Boston:
Boston University Center on Work and Family, 1995.

Scharlach, A. E., Lowe, B. F., and Schneider, E. L. *Elder Care and the Workforce.* San Francisco: New Lexington Press, 1991.

Thomas, L. T., and Ganster, D. C. "Impact of Family-Supportive Work Variables on Work-
Family Conflict and Strain: A Control Perspective." *Journal of Applied Psychology,* 1995,
80 (1), 6–15.

Trocki, K. F., and Orioli, E. M. "Gender Differences in Stress Symptoms, Stress-Producing
Contexts, and Coping Strategies." In G. Keita and J. Hurrell, Jr. (eds.), *Job Stress in a
Changing Workforce: Investigating Gender, Diversity, and Family Issues.* Washington, D.C.:
American Psychology Association, 1994.

U.S. Bureau of Labor Statistics. *Employment and Earnings.* Washington, D.C.: U.S. Department of Labor, January, 1998, 45 (1), 162–163.

U.S. Department of Labor. *1993 Handbook of Women Workers: Trends and Issues.* Washington, D.C.: U.S. Department of Labor Women's Bureau, 1994.

Waldfogel, J. "Working Mothers Then and Now: A Cross-Cohort Analysis of the Effects of
Maternity Leave on Women's Pay." In F. D. Blau and R. G. Ehrenberg (eds.), *Gender and
Family Issues in the Workplace.* New York: Russell Sage Foundation, 1997.

ROSE MARY WENTLING *is professor and coordinator of human resource development
in the Department of Human Resource Education, University of Illinois, Champaign.*

Increasing numbers of women in middle and later life remain employed in the workplace due to shifting social and economic structures, changing attitudes and expectations about women's careers, inadequate financial resources, and increased longevity. This chapter explores how these issues affect women's careers in later life, workplace challenges, and the opportunities for career development.

Women's Career Development in Midlife and Beyond

Vivian W. Mott

By now, the news that we are among an aging population is met with barely a raised brow. We know, for example, that the number of Americans over age eighty-five is expected nearly to double, from approximately 3 million in 1990 to more than 5 million shortly after the turn of the century (U.S. Bureau of the Census, 1992) and that between now and the year 2030, the baby boom generation will increasingly number among the young-old (Bee, 1996). We know, too, that women are among those on the front lines of this aging boom because they represent the majority of elderly, with the number of women over age sixty-five swelling from 18.5 million in 1990 to nearly 40 million by the year 2050 (Taeuber and Allen, 1993).

But what constitutes the older woman? Bee (1996) categorizes midlifers and the elderly according to four age ranges. Those who are between the ages of forty and sixty-five, she refers to being in *middle adulthood,* those between sixty-five and seventy-five the *young-old,* and those between seventy-five and eighty-five the *middle-old.* And with so many elderly now living into their ninth and tenth decades, a subsequent category is now that of the *oldest-old,* or those beyond the age of eighty-five. Because the focus of this chapter is career development of women in middle and later life, the age of interest will be forty-five and beyond. Three factors provide a rationale for this marker age. First, women near the age of forty-five are among those born during the middle years of the baby boom and are widely recognized as entering midlife. Second, women beyond the age of forty-five constitute a major segment of the workforce. And third, in spite of recent legislation offering legal protection, age discrimination is still a disturbing factor for women even in their forties, and thus affects their career development options. Thus, in a

New Directions for Adult and Continuing Education, no. 80, Winter 1998 © Jossey-Bass Publishers period of unprecedented social, economic, and technological change marked by knowledge obsolescence and career fluidity, women's career development in middle to later life is all the more important.

A caveat is in order, however. This range of age for women's career development—beyond the age of forty-five and perhaps extending as much as twenty-five years—is an extremely broad category for any discussion of merit. For this reason alone, it is important to remember that women in this broad age range are extremely heterogeneous. Not only do they represent different racial and ethnic origins, with their ages spanning as much as twenty-five years or more, but also they differ in educational attainment, socioeconomic status, attitudes about personal and professional lives, health status, and needs for career development. This chapter includes an overview of midlife women in today's workforce, an exploration of challenges and opportunities in women's career development, and discussion of implications for midlife women, educators, organizations, institutions, and society.

Midlife Women in the Workforce

In 1950 only 27 percent of women between the ages of fifty-five and sixty-four were in the workforce; by 1985 the percentage had climbed to 42 percent (Fullerton, 1992). In 1996 *Labor Review Monthly* projected that more than 50 percent of women in midlife and beyond—more than 5.5 million women—would remain in or rejoin the workforce (Besl and Kale, 1996). At the same time the number of employed men in this age range is decreasing. There are three reasons that more, not fewer, women remain employed. First, women in their middle and later lives are more likely to live alone and be in poor health, having survived their spouse or partner. Second, because of consistently disparate income and interrupted work lives, women are less likely than men to have adequate pensions, retirement accounts, and health care, and are thus more likely in need of supplemental income. And third, women in midlife may expect to live another twenty-five years or more.

In spite of the increases in participation of women in typically male-oriented and -dominated career fields, women of all ages remain underrepresented in skilled career fields due to misconceptions regarding gender-specific abilities and preferences and undervaluation of women's skills. According to Rayman, Allshouse, and Allen (1993), "The majority of [female] professional workers (56 percent) are found in two lower-paying categories—teachers (except for college and university) and registered nurses" (pp. 137–138). Interest in education and health career fields remains high, particularly for older women (Henderson, 1994). Women continue to be disproportionately employed in low-paying career fields that are projected to grow slowly, if at all. For instance, of the more than 60 percent of midlife white women who hold white- or pink-collar jobs, many remain clustered in low-level administrative positions, sales, and service careers. Although there exists little documentation on the careers of Asian and Hispanic women, more than 65 percent of black women work in service and information careers, with the majority of elderly black women found predominantly in private households (Perkins, 1993). Many of these career fields offer minimal retirement or health care benefits and equally deficient educational opportunities. Even in jobs or careers with higher salaries and opportunities for career development, women are often among the last to be offered such opportunities, many of which deal only with skill refinement rather than education to further advancement in the field or job setting.

Retirement also plays an important role in women's career patterns in middle and later life. Perkins found, for example, that "working class women who are involuntarily retired are more likely to return to work for economic reasons" (1993, p. 132) than those who leave voluntarily or who have planned for retirement. Reasons for involuntary retirement include health (frequently of spouse, partner, parent, or sibling), organizational changes in management or scope of work, or perceived discrimination. Ironically, women who return to work due to insufficient economic resources in retirement return to similar low-paying, gender-specific jobs, frequently for less money than they earned in the past.

Education as well has played a major role in the increased labor participation rates of midlife women. Although many women beyond the age of sixty have less education, the improved educational attainment of women between the ages of forty-five and sixty generally means better jobs and higher incomes than ever before. Since 1980, for example, women earned the majority of undergraduate and master's degrees and nearly half of all professional certifications and doctorates in the United States (National Center for Educational Statistics, 1995). Education and training will continue to play a crucial role for midlife women in their career development. Given their economic vulnerability and typical career participation patterns, many midlife women are able to improve their economic positions only through career shifts and advancement within established careers.

Opportunities and Challenges in the Workforce

The workplace is not an arbitrarily hostile place for women in midlife and beyond. After a decade or so of right-sizing, precarious funding, and increasing global competition, employers need not only qualified but also flexible and well-trained employees. Given the experiences, perspectives, and typical stability of midlife women, today's workplace offers unique opportunities for these women. Many employers find mature women valuable assets in the workplace: as excellent role models and supervisors for younger employees, as conscientious and motivated workers, and as stable and mindful employees who can identify with and respond to the client or customer base of the organization. In addition, the aging baby boomers provide a new perspective of midlife aging—one of vitality, experience, and enviable work ethics. Finally, as many women tire of the typical patriarchal environment of today's workplace, some find that midlife may be an ideal time to change careers or launch new ones. In fact, women are founding the majority of new small businesses, and women in midlife and beyond number significantly among the most successful of these new entrepreneurs.

Many of the challenges women face in their middle and later life career development are brought about not only by the quickly shifting knowledge base and dependence on technology, but also by the inherent patriarchal nature of the workplace. Women returning to the workforce after even two or three years of absence face challenges of rusty or obsolete skills and the competition of skilled workers ten to fifteen years younger. These obstacles are frequently met with negative attitudes and erroneous perceptions about women. The underrating of the importance of women's careers, of their need and desire for career education and training, of their understanding or propensity for things technological, and even of their abilities and energy level is still prevalent among many executives. As a result, older women experience a lack of support from many male supervisors in terms of appropriate role models and training opportunities, as well as subtle exclusion from informal social relationships that foster professional growth. Thus, despite minimal advances into career fields previously unavailable to women, many older women in particular are still constrained into a narrow band of the wider career spectrum that men enjoy, with the opportunities for mentoring, education, training, and career development still limited.

These career stereotypes and inequalities are reproduced as early as elementary and middle school and also during professional preparation programs. Apple (1979) argues, for instance, that the tradition associated with certain career fields is actually a manifestation of the dominant culture and requisite knowledge being transmitted in our schools. Older women in the workforce are particularly affected since the tradition that Apple wrote of was not even questioned, much less addressed, throughout most of their schooling and professional tenure. The situation is global, and there has been little apparent change since Apple wrote in 1979. Following her ethnographic study of the culture of an Australian university and its impact on the workplace, Patricia Weeks noted that the "masculine ethos of [education] erects barriers to women's full participation" (1992, p. 133). As an illustration, she cites the still insignificant numbers of women, particularly older women, who enter or are promoted in technological, scientific, and other typically male-dominated career fields. Weeks suggests that only as more women are educated and succeed in career fields that offer reward and advancement parallel to men's will their social, professional, and economic vulnerability lessen.

Women's Career Development in Midlife

The roles of professional preparation, continuing education, and training are crucial aspects of career development for all workers because of the rapidly changing nature of the workplace, increasing dependence on technology, and quickening obsolescence of our knowledge base. These issues, coupled with the increased economic vulnerability of women in midlife and beyond, make education and training especially important for the older female careerist.

Career and Training Patterns. In the past older women have been over-represented in part-time, temporary, and short-term jobs. Such noncontinuous work histories and the growing tendency toward women-owned small businesses frequently result in minimal access to education and training in the workplace and pose serious implications for career development opportunities as women age.

The increasingly higher costs of workplace education and training have a multiplying effect on older career women. With their resources limited to begin with, many personnel and human resource managers focus their limited training dollars on younger workers. According to research, however, midlife career women are found to have higher aspirations relative to their careers (Badenhoop and Johansen, 1980; Pickering and Galvin-Schaeters, 1988), and those with higher levels of education tend to remain in the workforce well beyond fifty years of age due to the higher opportunity cost or potentially higher income lost with increasing years of education (Besl and Kale, 1996). In countering the misconceptions of her needs, interests, and abilities in regard to workplace education, the older career woman may have to reassert her interest in technology, career changes, and retraining, while reminding the organization of the significant contribution and number of years she potentially has remaining in the career field and cautioning against negative and discriminatory perceptions about older careerists. Of course, midlife women are protected somewhat from age discrimination in regard to training and promotion, but organizations and institutions themselves can address inequities in career opportunities in a manner compatible with organizational mission and strategic plans. Organizations can address these issues by recognizing the trends toward more, not fewer, midlife women in the workforce, focusing training dollars in areas that support both organizational and employee goals, mentoring midlife women in responsible positions, and rewarding employees whose efforts further both their own personal goals and those of the organization.

Types of Career Development Sought. Women frequently cite the inadequacy of earlier opportunities for professional preparation programs (Mott, 1998; Poole and Nielsen, 1994). For these women, life choices, education limitations, or gender differentiation in career counseling contribute to restricted career paths and inadequate skills that affect career advancement. In a study of management promotion among men and women ages thirty-nine to sixty in Australia, Gold and Pringle (1989) noted the slight rise of women in male-dominated fields of management. Among the factors identified as critical in achieving promotion by the women in their study were assistance or coaching, training and experience, conscientious work ethics, and networking. The primary factor perceived as hindering women's chances for promotion was "organizational attitudes to women/being female in a male world" (p. 20).

In their study of seventy-six midlife homemakers who returned to the workforce after an absence of three years or more, Pickering and Galvin-Schaeters (1988) reported that the women perceived a lack of supervisory support and mentoring, and they experienced significant role strain and conflict, as well as reduced levels of self-esteem, autonomy, and assertiveness. Their high need for achievement, however, led them to seek out training opportunities for leadership and managerial skills, as well as interpersonal skills (including assertion, self-confidence, and time management). Shapiro and Fitzsimmons (1991) also suggest that women benefit not only from career development but counseling as well. Among the areas of focus that their studies indicate as advantageous are goal-setting skills and problem-solving strategies; assertiveness training, decision making, and communication skills; and group counseling wherein women might benefit from others' experiences in life and career coping skills.

Finally, other more personal areas of education are important to women in midlife careers. Many career women find themselves in the sandwich generation, caring for both dependent children (and perhaps even grandchildren) and parents in need of their assistance. According to some research, career women often face psychological challenges, such as isolation and vulnerability, as a result of behavioral compromises in their professional and private lives (Fisher, 1989). And while elderly women in particular face the most severe of economic and health disadvantages in their later years, the majority of all older career women are more likely to suffer from chronic health problems and frequently have inadequate health care options (Block and Gelfand, 1983; Brown, 1988). Therefore, stress management, health maintenance, and financial planning are three additional areas of education that would benefit the career development of women in midlife careers.

Given what is known of women's learning and development models (see, for example, Belenky, Clinchy, Goldberger, and Tarule, 1996; Gilligan, 1982; Taylor and Marienau, 1995), experiential forms of learning—observation and modeling, internships and apprenticeships, and team work projects—are perhaps among the most advantageous means to women's career development. Mentoring is another crucial career development opportunity for women. Unfortunately, there is a void of mentoring opportunities for most women due to persistent and negative misconceptions regarding women and work, the limited availability of appropriate role models, and apprehension and fear of sexual harassment charges on the part of mentors.

Much of women's career development, however, is necessarily self-directed and approached creatively. Career counselors suggest that in interviews, midlife women careerists should emphasize their recent accomplishments, creative and innovative projects (being very specific with details of project management), and ability to relate to a broader base of the organization's clientele. And midlife women who are seeking to reenter or shift careers are advised to engage in current, even if short-term, training in a field of urgent need; maintain current certifications and licenses as well as knowledge in their professional literature; maintain or renew professional networks and contacts with other women in similar career fields; consider participating in job readiness or career counseling programs at local community colleges; or consider a volunteer or part-time position in a field they want to pursue.

Available Resources. Many sponsored programs exist to aid women in midlife and beyond in their return to or advancement in the workplace. Programs operated by federal, state, and local agencies in every state assist underemployed women as well as the unemployed. And the Workforce Investment Act, passed by Congress in 1996, will provide additional opportunities in the coming years. In related efforts, many communities have adult resource centers that provide academic and career counseling as well as guidance regarding personal issues of concern to older career women (Henderson, 1994).

Another innovative means of staying current or learning new career skills are the many Centers for Learning in Retirement in more than 150 colleges and universities. These centers, designed specifically for older learners, are often organized and managed exclusively by the center members who are especially sensitive to the issues and concerns of those participating in their programs. Also, there exists a plethora of publications available for career guidance for older women careerists, among them publications by the American Association of Retired Persons (AARP) such as *How to Stay Employable: A Guide for the Mid-life and Older Worker* (1994). *AARP WORKS* (http://www.aarp.org) participants (more women than men) take part in eight sessions, which include self-guided assessments in interests and abilities, workshops on résumé writing and interview skills, and networking opportunities with employers and careerists in a variety of career fields that might be of interest to potential job seekers.

Implications for the Future

The picture of women in middle and later life in the workplace in need of and seeking relevant, rewarding, and ongoing career development is complex. Although they represent a crucial and expanding segment of the workplace of the next century, women age forty-five and over are undervalued in the workplace, underrepresented in careers that offer adequate incomes and benefit packages, and often overlooked when it comes to education, training, and career development. Policymakers and executives must recognize the demographic trends and strive for a workplace that is equitable, intellectually stimulating, and psychologically inviting. Educators, human resource managers, and counselors also play a significant role in helping ensure that the workplace is supportive of all older careerists by planning and implementing career development programs that are sensitive to aging and other issues of diversity.

Older women are aware of the fluidity of today's work environment; they are committed to career development and desire a wide variety of training opportunities that are easily transferred across settings. Opportunities exist for policymakers, executives in business and industry, human resource managers, adult educators, career counselors, and the women careerists themselves to help ensure that extended career years are years of promise, contribution, and reward for women in midlife and beyond.

References

American Association of Retired Persons. *How to Stay Employable: A Guide for the Mid-life and Older Worker.* Washington, D.C.: American Association of Retired Persons, 1994.

American Association of Retired Persons. *AARP WORKS: Information Resources for Members.* Washington, D.C.: American Association of Retired Persons, 1998. [http://www.aarp.org].

Apple, M. *Ideology and Curriculum.* New York: Routledge, 1979.

Badenhoop, M. S., and Johansen, M. K. "Do Reentry Women Have Special Needs?" *Psychology of Women Quarterly,* 1980, *4* (4), 591–595.

Bee, H. L. *The Journey of Adulthood.* (3rd ed.) Englewood Cliffs, N.J.: Prentice Hall, 1996.

Belenky, M. F., Clinchy, B. M., Goldberger, N. R., and Tarule, J. M. *Women's Ways of Knowing: The Development of Self, Voice, and Mind.* New York: Basic Books, 1996.

Besl, J. R., and Kale, B. D. "Older Workers in the 21st Century, Active and Educated: A Study." *Monthly Labor Review,* June 1996, pp. 18–26.

Block, M., and Gelfand, D. *Health Concerns of Older Women.* Working Paper, no. 4. Baltimore: University of Maryland, National Policy Center on Women and Aging, 1983.

Brown, R. D. *Employment and Wealth Among Older Black Women: Implications for Their Economic Status.* Working Paper, no. 77. Wellesley, Mass.: Wellesley College, Center for Research on Women, 1988.

Fisher, A. B. *Wall Street Women: Women in Power on Wall Street Today.* New York: Knopf, 1989.

Fullerton, H. N. "Labor Force Projections: The Baby Boom Moves On." In *Outlook: 1990–2005.* BLS Bulletin 2402. Washington, D.C.: U.S. Government Printing Office, 1992.

Gilligan, C. *In a Different Voice: Psychological Theory and Women's Development.* Cambridge, Mass.: Harvard University Press, 1982.

Gold, J. O., and Pringle, J. K. "Gender-Specific Factors in Management Promotion." *Journal of Management Psychology,* 1989, *3* (4), 17–22.

Henderson, C. *Labor Force Participation of Older College Graduates.* Washington, D.C.: American Council of Education, Division of Policy Analysis and Research, 1994. (ED 381 680)

Mott, V. W. "Meaning-Making in Mid and Late Adulthood: Case Studies of Women in Retirement." Paper presented at the Association for Gerontology in Higher Education Annual Conference, Winston-Salem, N.C., Feb. 19–22, 1998.

National Center for Education Statistics. *Statistics in Brief: Forty Percent of Adults Participate in Adult Education Activities: 1994–1995.* Washington, D.C.: U.S. Department of Education, Office of Educational Research and Improvement, Nov. 1995.

Perkins, K. "Working-Class Women and Retirement." *Journal of Gerontological Social Work,* 1993, *20* (3/4), 129–146.

Pickering, G. S., and Galvin-Schaeters, K. "An Empirical Study of Reentry Women." *Journal of Counseling Psychology,* 1988, *35* (3), 298–303.

Poole, M. E., and Nielsen, S. W. "Women's Career Development: Barriers to Learning within the Traditional Workplace." Paper presented at the American Educational Research Association Conference, New Orleans, Apr. 1994. (ED 374 250)

Rayman, P., Allshouse, K., and Allen, J. "Resiliency Amidst Inequity: Older Women Workers in an Aging United States." In J. Allen and A. Pifer (eds.), *Women on the Front Lines.* Washington, D.C.: Urban Institute Press, 1993.

Shapiro, M., and Fitzsimmons, G. "Women Preparing to Re-enter the Workforce." *Canadian Journal of Counselling,* 1991, *25* (4), 510–519.

Taeuber, C. M., and Allen, J. "Women in Our Aging Society: The Demographic Outlook." In J. Allen and A. Pifer (eds.), *Women on the Front Lines.* Washington, D.C.: Urban Institute Press, 1993.

Taylor, K., and Marienau, C. (eds.). *Learning Environments for Women's Adult Development: Bridges toward Change.* New Directions for Adult and Continuing Education, no. 65. San Francisco: Jossey-Bass, 1995.

U.S. Bureau of the Census. *1990 United States Census.* Washington, D.C.: U.S. Government Printing Office, 1992.

Weeks, P. "Women into Trades: Rhetoric or Reality?" In M. E. Poole (ed.), *Education and Work.* Hawthorn, Victoria: Australian Council for Educational Research, 1992.

VIVIAN W. MOTT is assistant professor in the Department of Counselor and Adult Education, East Carolina University, Greenville, North Carolina.

The glass ceiling in organizational life is a reality. Nevertheless, there are strategies women can use to get the recognition and rewards they deserve at work.

Women's Career Development at the Glass Ceiling

Patricia L. Inman

The glass ceiling is an invisible barrier that prevents women from moving beyond middle management into positions of senior executive status. The term itself was coined in 1986 as a result of a three-year study, supported by the Center for Creative Leadership, that looked at seventy-six female executives and their male associates at America's top companies (Morrison, White, Van Velsor, and the Center for Creative Leadership, 1987). The study concluded that the glass ceiling functioned as a significant barrier to women's advancement. One of the findings was that certain behaviors acceptable for men were viewed as unacceptable for women. For instance, political action was tolerated in men, but women were disparaged for employing similar tactics. This double standard was largely ignored in corporate contexts, and many women chose to leave corporations rather than stay and mitigate it. The study offered the following advice for women who sought success: put in extra time and effort, advertise your abilities, cultivate allies, and actively seek opportunities.

How have women fared in light of this advice? Have they gained ground in entering corporate leadership positions and breaking the glass ceiling? Considering compensation for male and female executives, large companies are closing the gap the fastest. But as the 1998 salary survey done by Working Women (Dogar, 1998) indicates, they had the largest gap to close in the first place. Women in small and midsize companies enjoy the most compensation equity, although their pay gains lag behind those of their colleagues in larger corporations. Salaries for female CEOs in the Fortune 1000 increased by 9 percent during 1996–1997, bringing their overall compensation to an average of $3 million. This is an encouraging figure until you compare it to the average income of a male Fortune 1000 CEO in 1997: $5.8 million. More important, a 1997 Catalyst survey found that women currently hold only 10.6 percent of all board of director seats in Fortune 500 companies (Dogar, 1998). So although women are closing the compensation gap, they often do not enjoy the status of creating policy.

The problem with the glass ceiling study is that it examined how women can succeed in a culture that praises and rewards traditional male-dominated approaches. The concept of breaking the glass ceiling as it was presented by the authors of the study is that it implied acceptance of the current male-centered corporate culture. Yet this tactic has not been effective. And with rapidly changing corporate contexts, this does not strengthen organizational performance for the long term.

Women have been asking the wrong question. The question is not how women can adjust to a male culture but how to change the prevailing corporate culture so that glass ceilings are shattered for all groups. Female leadership roles will evolve through the creative evolution of an organic corporate culture that allows talent and the resulting varied leadership styles to emerge. Working within an alienated organizational culture can result only in minimizing individual potential. Palmer (1983) tells us that the foundation for any culture lies in the way it answers the question, "Where do reality and power reside?" (p. 19). This chapter proposes that success for women lies not in adaptation to a foreign reality, as has been suggested in past strategies for breaking the glass ceiling. Rather, power resides in that which is unique to each individual—a collection of diverse gifts formerly denied. This is especially true for women whose gendered voice is often silenced. These recommendations fly in the face of strategies of accommodation.

Today's Corporate Context

To see how organizations have changed, one must look at the increasing diversity of the workforce with its incremental potential; the world's shift from an industrial to an information society as it joins the global economy; the blurring of public and private lives as women, who continue to be responsible for the majority of home and family tasks, enter the workforce in increasing numbers; and the pervasive spirit of instability as corporations continue to downsize in their attempt to function more effectively.

Increasing Diversity of the Workforce. A compelling argument for corporate change was presented in *Workforce 2000*, a report by the Hudson Institute, which indicated that the composition of the workforce of the future would be much different from that of 1987, when this study was completed. By the year 2000, it was projected that only 15 percent would be native white men; the rest would be native white women (42 percent), native nonwhite women (13 percent) and men (7 percent), and immigrant men (13 percent) and women (9 percent). These data alone should convince corporate managers to advocate for diversity. Further, a Covenant Investment Management study of the Standard and Poor's 500 revealed that the stock performance of companies that encouraged diversity in the workplace was 2.4 times higher than the performance of firms that did not (Gold, 1998).

Emphasis on the Learning Process. In *Everyday Revolutionaries: Working Women and the Transformation of American Life,* Sally Helgesen (1998) presents an explanation for this positive effect of diversity within the workplace. Helgesen asserts that the postindustrial organization, with its emphasis on the value of knowledge and information, must recognize the need to draw talent from a broader base. The author makes the point that organizations have become too competitive to tolerate exclusionary policies. Therefore, the recommendation made by Morrison, White, Van Velsor, and the Center for Creative Leadership (1987) to "cultivate allies" becomes less significant in breaking the glass ceiling.

Peter Drucker (1994) documents this emerging emphasis on knowledge and its effect on organizational development. Globally we have moved from an agrarian, to an industrial, to a knowledge society. Knowledge has become the key resource. According to Drucker, knowledge workers gain access to jobs and social position through formal education. But informal knowledge—acquired outside of institutional structure—is as important in this type of organization (Marsick and Watkins, 1993). This is particularly significant for women, who bring varied life experiences to the workplace. The implication is that how well one acquires and applies knowledge is a key factor in a person's success rather than strength or political connections. Drucker states, "In the knowledge society, for the first time in history, the possibility of leadership is open to all" (1994, p. 67).

With this change of focus to the learning process, the definition of an educated person has changed as well from an individual with a prescribed stock of linear knowledge to a person who has learned how to learn and continues to learn throughout life.

The Blurring of Public and Private Lives. Current technology supports returning work to the home. This factor is especially significant for the increasing number of women who are serving in management roles of increasing levels of responsibility. At all levels of employment, research has shown that women spend more hours on work and family tasks than men do (Friedman, 1992). As technology frees individuals from the physical site of the workplace, the barriers of work and home have begun to erode, returning the corporate environment "to an earlier more integrated conception of life's meaning and purpose" (Helgesen, 1998, p. 57). With corporations realizing that they must link family issues with the bottom line, the workplace is being reshaped, with lines between life spheres blurring.

This change brings into question the suggestion by Morrison, White, Van Velsor, and the Center for Creative Leadership (1987) to "put in extra time and effort." Additional effort would still seem appropriate, but it becomes more important to follow one of the other directives—"advertise your abilities"—as one makes a conscious effort to document work-related effort expended outside the workplace.

Pervasive Corporate Instability. With the trend to downsize and streamline management, employees have been forced to reassess their role within individual organizations. Career strategies are much more entrepreneurial as individuals realize the importance of developing and marketing themselves rather than their position.

Women have a long tradition of moving in and out of the workplace in order to care for aging parents; they generally feel less stigma than men when they have taken periods off; with less seniority, women have less job security and so often have been the first casualties of downsizing; they have been driven from large organizations at a faster rate than men by the persistence of the glass ceiling; they are more likely than men to seek retraining on their own time and using their own money. Thus, some of the very disadvantages that held women back in the industrial workplace are now often proving advantageous enabling women to the realities of the information economy, and pushing them to improvise individual solutions to the pervasive instability that confronts us all [Helgesen, 1998, pp. 46–47].

Women's Leadership. In *Reinventing the Corporation* (1985) Aburdene and Naisbitt searched for examples of a new breed of manager needed for the organizations of the future—leaders who could "create a nourishing environment for personal growth" so necessary for a newly diversified workforce who functioned within the information society that had recently emerged in the global economy. Many authors advised women to imitate "male" strategies based on control and competition, but the old way of managing did not seem to be working for anyone.

Rosner (1990) studied male and female executives with similar jobs, education, and ages and concluded that women and men manage quite differently. Women, honoring unique talent, try to transform people's self-interest into organizational goals. Helgesen (1990) and Grant (1988) have also documented such organic leadership. Further Cafferella, Clark, and Ingram (1997) completed a significant study of female middle managers within corporations that supported the fact that women in leadership roles "focused on the importance of participation, collaborative interaction and knowing and embracing the different styles of their people" (p. 92), which are so important in allowing individual potential to develop within organizations. Many of the attributes for which women's leadership is praised are rooted in women's socialized roles. The traditional female value of caring for others, balanced with sufficient objectivity, is the basis of the management skill of supporting and encouraging people and bringing out their best (Aburdene and Naisbitt, 1992). Corporations are slow in identifying these skills that women bring to the organization, and women would be well advised to advertise such abilities.

Career Strategies

The question then becomes: How do women get the recognition they deserve while working in a culture that praises and rewards the more traditional, male-dominated approaches?

Know Thyself. The success of the organic model of leadership builds on the uniqueness of diverse styles and talents and depends on knowing oneself and teaching others how to self-assess. In their 1997 study Cafferella, Clark, and Ingram found that women exhibited leadership styles that reflected the qualities often specific to women and so appropriate to today's corporate context (Grant, 1988), yet female leaders often showed a remarkable lack of awareness of these qualities. Grant argues that qualities such as affiliation, attachment, cooperativeness, nurturance, and emotionality that support the architecture of the new organization are culturally developed in women. Susan Wittig Albert (1997) emphasizes the individual use of journaling and other forms of narrative to document such talents. These narrative assessments serve as a map of the learning process and self-definition and help to transfer learning assessment from the organization to the individual.

Acknowledging strengths includes the permission to use intuition in decision making. Intuition here is defined as knowledge attained through the senses that is stored in the unconscious. Strong (1994) found that although women have more highly developed intuitive knowledge than men, they are hesitant to use this skill because they feel the need to explain their decision in rational terms. In contrast, men base decisions more frequently on "hunches," although these are more frequently ill advised.

Because it is so difficult for women to accept gendered leadership characteristics in an alien culture, it is important for women to surround themselves with those who know and celebrate what they can do, not what they cannot. Women must give themselves permission to achieve at all organizational levels. Often those who care about them the most are the ones who do not wish them to take risks and possibly fail. Women must seek out those who will encourage them to develop their potential to the fullest.

Develop Multiple Mentors. Once they have addressed the issues of discovery of talents and permission to use them, women need to address strategies to strengthen the areas that are essential to individual development. In the past a single personal mentor was often all that an employee needed to make the proper political connections; now they must be able to choose multiple mentors and both formal and informal strategies to extend capabilities. Autonomous development of skills, technical or social, is essential to career development. Whereas Morrison, White, Van Velsor, and the Center for Creative Leadership (1987) advise "cultivating allies," the goal of choosing mentors now is to further skills rather than to cultivate political allies.

In the study by Cafferella, Clark, and Ingram (1997) women working in leadership roles just below the glass ceiling "all described an experience or cluster of experiences that contributed significantly to their development and self-confidence" (p. 91). Women must develop personal learning webs, which include both formal and informal experiences. In the case of informal learning, it also becomes important to find ways to document and validate such experience. This supports the original advice for breaking the glass ceiling to "advertise your abilities." Now, women should feel comfortable advertising the abilities that are characteristically theirs.

Although leadership styles unique to women have been documented (Rosner, 1990), each woman must master her own approach; there is no one female leadership model. One way to begin is to study the examples of successful women, as well as male mentors and teachers who have inspired one, and adopt those behaviors that have proved effective.

Integrate Body and Soul. Finally, Cafferella, Clark, and Ingram (1997) and Helgesen (1998) found that women in higher levels of leadership paid a high personal price for success. I suggest that society has conspired against women in this respect, particularly with its emphasis on the nuclear family. Women report almost twice as many work-family conflicts as men do, with their resulting impact of increasing difficulty concentrating on either work *or* family life (Rogers and others, 1988). Helgesen (1998) suggests that women need to develop and use community resources in the effort to integrate work and family lives—for example, cooperative child care arrangements, which can assist flexible work schedules, informal learning groups, and supportive religious affiliations. Networking to develop these supports becomes crucial.

This strategy follows Morrison, White, Van Velsor, and the Center for Creative Leadership's (1987) advice to "cultivate allies." However, rather than the political allies they have in mind, these allies provide for peace of mind, which can result in job enhancement. This is a double-edged sword. Uncovering resources within the community requires devoting time to such structures. So although personal development is important, the development of community is too, and this takes time to cultivate.

Develop Fluid and Customized Careers. Women should take advantage of their ability to customize their careers. Due to their ability to shift focus in the course of a lifetime, women have a capability to shift jobs and careers, which can support career development. According to Helgesen (1998) women are more likely to start their own businesses, telecommute, assume work on a project basis, work from home, integrate periods of education with periods of employment, and plan for longer work lives punctuated by periods away from work. In workplaces where predictable patterns of employment are no longer effective, this talent is particularly adaptive; all women should develop and cultivate innovative ways of working. In *Composing a Life,* Bateson (1990) documents this unique source of wisdom. Referring specifically to the discontinuities that have emerged in the shifting business and industrial environment, she urges women "to explore the creative potential of interrupted and conflicted lives, where energies are not narrowly focused or permanently pointed to a single ambition. These are not lives without commitment, but rather lives in which commitments are continually refocused and redefined" (p. 9).

Indeed, many women are finding that the very skills that have not been valued in the past have helped them find creative ways of breaking the glass ceiling or, and possibly more important, have caused women to question whether such an intense career pattern is necessary for "success" in life.

Although this strategy follows Morrison, White, Van Velsor, and the Center for Creative Leadership's (1987) advice to "actively seek opportunities" in the current corporate situation, it might be more appropriate to suggest that women "actively create opportunities." Numerous career possibilities exist, sometimes limited only by the ability to imagine productive alternatives.

Future Directions for Research

In most corporate cultures today, reality and power lie in the external world of objects and events and in the objective sciences that study the world. Personal or spiritual connection within the workplace is a romantic fantasy that impedes rather than enhances performance. I am convinced that corporations perpetuate this myth out of ignorance. Male-dominated corporate cultures judge women through male lenses, resulting in discrimination that at times is invisible to those in power. It is left to women to disclose the new corporate reality and the resulting "female advantage" through research encompassing new images.

Howard Becker (1998) has looked at innovative research practices to unshroud such radical truths and believes that in the past, research looked for causes rather than connections. He suggests that we instead develop narrative forms of research that document a history or story that asks, How did we come to this place? Who did what, and how does this culture exist as it does? Becker feels that only by looking at the history of cultures can we realize how they continue to exist even beyond their effectiveness. Becker's suggestions for new ways of thinking about research support Aburdene and Naisbitt's (1992) call to women in leadership roles to address "not only . . . issues of organizational culture but . . . also . . . the organization's relationship to women and the attendant myths" (p. 107).

Conclusion

Today's transformed organizations would benefit greatly from the leadership skills often associated with women (affiliation, attachment, cooperativeness, and nurturance); nevertheless, the command-and-control corporate culture continues to minimize the effectiveness of such diverse leadership skills. Therefore, career development strategies place much more responsibility on women to define and develop individual talents. Jane Martin Roland (1994) echoes this need to reshape the turf of the workplace in the struggle to validate women's particular knowledge. She identifies the messages that still clearly ring in many workplaces. "You are welcome to walk on our turf, but kindly obey the rules: (1) Keep within its borders. (2) Do not alter its shape. (3) Do not plant your own ideas. (4) Do not leave your mark" (p. 126). She urges women not to forsake their own values and opinions in an attempt to fit into a questionable mold.

I end with a word of caution. Women must not achieve corporate success at the expense of economic polarization. While we celebrate the fact that a greater number of women have reached advanced corporate levels with resulting compensation, we must be cautious of the increasing influence of affluence with its exclusionary practices directed to those who have not made it to the top. Women who have found corporate success must not feel the need to differentiate themselves from those being left behind in highly volatile corporate environments. Rather, I suggest a more collegial support and nurturance for women still struggling for economic security.

This increasing emphasis on affluence has increased the demand for privacy and private services to the detriment of community. Increased commitment to the workplace leaves one with less time for the development of community. We must not lose our perspective as women that connections in humanity are ever precious.

References

Aburdene, P., and Naisbitt. *Megatrends for Women: From Liberation to Leadership.* New York: Fawcett Columbine, 1992.

Albert, S. W. *Writing from Life: Telling Your Soul's Story.* New York: Putman, 1994.

Bateson, Mary Catherine. *Composing a Life.* New York: Penguin Books, 1990.

Becker, H. *Tricks of the Trade: How to Think About Your Research While You're Doing It.* Chicago: University of Chicago Press, 1998.

Cafferella, R., Clark, C., and Ingram, P. "Life at the Glass Ceiling: Women in Mid-Level Management Positions." In *27th Annual SCUTREA Conference Proceedings 1997.*

Dogar, D. "Nineteenth Annual Salary Report." *Working Woman,* Feb. 1998, pp. 23–25.

Drucker, P. "The Age of Social Transformation." *Atlantic Monthly,* Nov. 1994, pp. 53–80.

Friedman, D. "Working Couples." Presentation to Baxter Healthcare, McGaw Park, Illinois, November 18, 1992.

Grant, J. "Women as Managers: What They Can Offer to Organizations." *Organizational Dynamics,* Winter 1988, pp. 56–63.

Held, V. *Feminist Morality: Transforming Culture, Society, and Politics.* Chicago: University of Chicago Press, 1993.

Helgesen, S. *The Female Advantage.* New York: Doubleday, 1990.

Helgesen, S. *Everyday Revolutionaries: Working Women and the Transformation of American Life.* New York: Doubleday, 1998.

Hudson Institute. *Workforce 2000.* Indianapolis, Ind.: Hudson Institute, 1987.

Marsick, V., and Watkins, K. *Sculpting the Learning Organization: Lessons in the Art and Science of Systematic Change.* San Francisco: Jossey-Bass, 1993.

Martin, J. R. *Changing the Educational Landscape: Philosophy, Women, and Curriculum.* New York: Routledge, 1994.

Morrison, A. M., White, R. P., Van Velsor, E., and Center for Creative Leadership. *Breaking the Glass Ceiling: Can Women Reach the Top of America's Largest Corporations?* Reading, Mass.: Addison-Wesley, 1987.

Palmer, P. *To Know as We Are Known: A Spirituality of Education.* San Francisco: Harper San Francisco, 1983.

Rosner, J. Research sponsored by the International Women's Forum published in the *Harvard Business Review,* November-December 1990.

Strong, R. "Journeys to Personal Power as a Basis for Decision Making for Continuing Educators." Unpublished doctoral dissertation, Northern Illinois University, 1994.

Walden, P. "Journal Writing: A Tool for Women Developing as Knowers." In K. Taylor and C. Marienu (eds.), *New Directions for Adult and Continuing Education,* no. 65. San Francisco: Jossey-Bass, 1995.

PATRICIA L. INMAN *is a faculty member of the College of Management and Business, National-Louis University, Chicago, Illinois.*

Voluntary part-time work arrangements offer benefits to both employees and employers. They also pose challenges to women who use them. Strategies for both supervisors and the women who use part-time arrangements are critical to success.

Women's Career Development and Part-Time Arrangements

Marcia Brumit Kropf

Voluntary, temporary, part-time work arrangements provide much needed support for the women who comprise 46 percent of the U.S. labor force and 49 percent of managerial and professional specialty positions (U.S. Bureau of Labor Statistics, 1998). These options of individually negotiated and formally reduced work schedules to part time on a weekly, monthly, annual, or project basis, including job sharing or telecommuting, affect salary, benefits, and professional advancement. It is critical for adult education programs, especially those focused on women, to explain these options, communicate their importance and impact, describe the challenges to career advancement, and teach individuals strategies and skills critical to success. Students in these programs need to understand part-time arrangements from a range of perspectives, because they can become employees using alternative arrangements, supervisors managing part-time employees, or employers implementing these arrangements in order to attract and retain women.

Women and Voluntary Part-Time Arrangements

Although voluntary part-time arrangements are increasingly of interest to men and women of all ages, they are currently used primarily by women with children, especially those with preschool-aged children. This is an important group for employers to consider because women with children comprise an increasing proportion of the labor force: 70 percent of women with children under age eighteen are employed; 40 percent of employed women are mothers of children under age eighteen (U.S. Bureau of Labor Statistics, 1996).

In a national study of 802 members of dual-career couples (Catalyst, 1998), 49 percent of the women had used a formal flexible work program of some kind, and 72 percent said that they would look for such programs in a new employer. In another survey with 1,105 respondents from four organizations, nearly one in four of the women (23 percent) currently had a part-time arrangement, and 36 percent expected to work part time at some point in their careers: they had worked part time in the past, were then working part time, or expected to work part time in the future (Catalyst, 1997). That study provided a profile of the typical professional with a voluntary part-time arrangement: median age of 39.7 years, 80 percent women, 96 percent married, 78 percent with a spouse employed full time, and 74 percent with children under the age of eighteen. The median tenure with the employer is 7.2 years.

These findings clarify both the significance of these arrangements to women and the relevance of educating women, as employees and as supervisors, about how to implement these arrangements effectively.

Need for Part-Time Arrangements

Women, as the primary caregivers in our society, often find the traditional structures for maintaining and advancing careers restricting and at odds with the responsibilities they have outside work (Catalyst, 1996b). The traditional career pathing structures in many organizations were designed for male employees with unemployed wives who handled outside-of-work responsibilities. These structures often require professionals and managers seeking advancement to honor "face time" in the office, travel extensively, relocate every few years, and focus exclusively on work responsibilities during the same life cycle stage when women are having children. In addition, today's demanding work environments frequently require professionals and managers to commit to constant availability and long work hours, beyond the traditional forty-hour, nine–to–five, Monday-to-Friday schedule. In fact, in some organizations today, women told Catalyst that they need a formal part-time work arrangement in order to ensure a forty-hour work week (1993). Some women continue their part-time arrangements, with reduced compensation, rather than working full time in order to ensure that they do not have to regularly work evenings and weekends and to allow themselves the flexibility to change their hours when needed.

Benefits of Part-Time Arrangements for Women

Women who participated in the Catalyst studies clearly understand that the choice of a part-time arrangement involves a slowdown in terms of career advancement. They use terms such as "on-hold career" or "career plateau." One woman noted, "Since I was not really intent on immediate promotion, this worked well for me. For a person who wants to advance quickly, within a year or two, flexible hours probably would not be the way to go" (Catalyst, 1993,

p. 34). Most often women use part-time arrangements as a way to avoid stepping away from the workplace altogether, a choice that also has serious career implications. Adult education programs can help women understand the benefits of these arrangements, allowing them to make informed decisions about working part time. Women in Catalyst studies describe a number of major benefits to choosing to work part time.

Maintaining Career Momentum. Many women are searching for ways to maintain a career and professional identity while being a parent. Using a part-time arrangement for a period of time allows women to stay in the workplace: "Our [she and her job-sharing partner] primary goal was not to advance right now because we knew what came with that: a lot of time and travel with little kids at home. We just knew that that wasn't what we wanted to do. So we both felt that for the time being we wanted to maintain a career and have responsible positions" (Catalyst, 1993, p. 36).

Maintaining a Professional Identity. In addition, women describe the need to maintain a professional identity that upholds their self-esteem: "Self-esteem, I think that was important. Working at the firm is a pretty prestigious thing, and I enjoyed that. I enjoyed getting paid well. I enjoyed intellectual and social companionship" (Catalyst, 1993, p. 36).

Continuing to Develop Skills and Professional Expertise. A reduced work arrangement, as opposed to leaving the workplace to stay home full time, allows for continued on-the-job learning and skill development: "The biggest benefit is that I've been able to keep my career in engineering going. If I'd taken these five years off and chosen to stay home with children, I'd be out of touch with all the things that are going on and obviously not able to come back at the level I was then or the one I'm at right now. It kept my career going" (Catalyst, 1993, p. 36).

Easing the Transition Back to Full-Time Work. Having a part-time arrangement, rather than leaving the workplace altogether while caring for family members, makes it easier for a woman to move back to full-time work when she is ready. Staying in the workforce enables her to maintain her professional network, continue to develop skills, and sustain a performance track record.

Building Economic Security. Part-time arrangements allow women to continue to build individual economic security. Although compensation is reduced in these arrangements, prorated to the reduction in work hours, maintaining a salary history and continuing contributions to social security and pensions are a major economic benefit. Career gaps are associated with lower career-long income (Schneer and Reitman, 1997).

Balancing Work and Caregiving Responsibilities. Women repeatedly describe the positive impact of part-time arrangements on their ability to balance time with their families and time for outside responsibilities. A part-time professional in a consulting firm described the impact: "I am much happier at work and at home. My child is happier. My marriage is stronger. My colleagues appreciate my new outlook on life. I was too stressed previously. Now I love working" (Catalyst, 1997, p. 81). Ninety-three percent of those with part-time arrangements in Catalyst's 1997 study reported feeling an increased ability to juggle work and family, and 74 percent of full-time employees agreed.

Benefits of Part-Time Arrangements for Employers

As the percentage of women in the professional and managerial workforce has increased, employers have begun to offer a range of programs and policies designed to attract, retain, and motivate this pool of talent. The trend is for more and more employers, primarily large corporations, to create flexible work arrangement policies for professionals and managers (Catalyst, 1996a). Adult education programs can educate students who are employers and supervisors about the tangible business benefits of these arrangements for employers.

Retaining Valuable, Experienced Employees. Women in Catalyst studies repeatedly describe their commitment to employers who enable them to work part time: "Because of the arrangement that was given to me, I have an incredible amount of loyalty to the firm just because they were helpful to me, considerate when I needed time, and I felt like I owed them something in return" (Catalyst, 1993, p. 32). In a recent survey (Catalyst, 1997), 78 percent of the 965 full-time employees and 98 percent of the 91 part-time employees responding agreed that offering flexible arrangements helps the employer retain valuable employees. And 37 percent of the part-time professionals said that the arrangement was essential for their continuing with their employers.

Increasing Morale and Productivity. Participants in Catalyst studies consistently report increases in morale, productivity, and quality of work when they work part time. Eighty percent of the survey respondents in the 1997 Catalyst survey reported increases in morale for individuals working part time or telecommuting, and 46 percent agreed that individuals working part time realize productivity gains. Typical comments from part-time employees included: "I really do so much more in three days than I did in five days" (Catalyst, 1997, p. 22).

Career Challenges for Women with Part-Time Arrangements

Although employers may have part-time work policies, Catalyst studies have repeatedly found that the mere existence of policies is not enough to ensure that these arrangements are available and used effectively. Many female employees find themselves approaching an unenlightened manager or employer to discuss a new conceptualization for how work can be done, designing arrangements without guidance or expertise, and piloting arrangements in unfriendly and uneducated work environments.

Women must understand the career challenges they face and the organizational barriers to be surmounted when working part time in organizations that promote a "work is all" set of values. A critical aspect of adult educational programs for women must be to describe and discuss these challenges, as well as to develop the understanding and skills to surmount them. Catalyst's 1996 guide, *Making Work Flexible: Policy to Practice,* describes these barriers in detail and provides strategies, with examples, for the effective implementation of flexible arrangements.

Being Viewed as Uncommitted. Work environment cultures value and reinforce the traditional ways that work has been defined. In many organizations, someone who works part time is seen as less committed and serious about career advancement by senior management, managers, and colleagues. This point of view may result in fewer developmental opportunities and critical assignments for the part-time worker.

Being Less Visible and Losing High-Profile Assignments. Traditionally work has been defined as occurring only in the workplace, where supervisors used a "line-of sight" model: they knew what work was being done and who was doing it because they could see it happening. Supervisors may make presumptions about the abilities of someone who is not in the office all the time. They may give important assignments to others without thinking or schedule important meetings during times when the part-time employee is out. Women who work part time may find themselves taken less seriously and losing touch with what is happening at work. One woman explained, "They didn't see us, so we must not be working. That was really the bottom line" (Catalyst, 1993, p. 27).

Losing Critical Responsibilities. Although there are many examples of successful part-time supervisors and client-service professionals, managers may assume that part-time arrangements are inappropriate for supervisory or client-based positions, requiring that women relinquish these assignments if they work part time. Yet these responsibilities are often critical experiences for advancement, and losing them can interfere with a woman's ability to move ahead.

Taking On Too Much Work. Many women are so pleased to have the opportunity to work part time that they do not negotiate reductions in their work assignments as well. Instead they focus on negotiating a reduced schedule and time away from the office. The result is that they have a reduced schedule (and reduced compensation) but continue to have full-time work responsibilities, and they do not achieve the primary goal of the arrangement: improved ability to balance work and home responsibilities. In the end, the women feel overwhelmed and may not be able to meet their work goals. The supervisors then may feel that work suffers, and colleagues may feel that the arrangement leaves them with additional work. In Catalyst's 1997 study, for example, 49 percent of the part-time employees reported no change in their workload and 12 percent reported an increase in workload. Their direct supervisors and colleagues agreed.

Strategies for Successful Part-Time Arrangements

These consequences can result in serious harm to a woman's career, especially because they limit assignments and responsibilities and she may not acquire experiences critical to advancement. Catalyst research has highlighted many examples of women who have worked part time and successfully avoided these negative consequences to their careers. The most critical activity is to engage in explicit and regular discussions with supervisors about long-term career goals and plans, the specifics of the arrangement and how to make it work, as well as work schedules, plans, and commitments.

Success Strategies for Supervisors. Adult education programs can make a major contribution by helping professionals develop as effective supervisors and managers. Catalyst research has clarified specific skills that supervisors of part-time employees need.

Be a Supportive Supervisor. All forty-five of the women in Catalyst's 1993 study described their supervisors as supportive. These supervisors accepted family concerns as a legitimate issue, understood the company's policies, and felt comfortable discussing work-family issues with their employees. Having a supportive supervisor is critical to having a part-time arrangement approved, to the success of the arrangement, and to the professional opportunities available while working part time.

Focus on Work and Productivity. Supervisors who describe behaviors critical to supporting flexible arrangements emphasize the importance of objectively focusing on the work at hand, reconceptualizing tasks in news ways, and designing concrete productivity measures rather than relying on time in the office. One supervisor explained: "We had to re-look at how we're doing our work. I brought the group together and said, 'What are your ideas about how we can make this work?'" (Catalyst, 1997, p. 71).

Rethink Supervisory Habits. Supervising employees with flexible work arrangements requires managers to reassess how they assign and plan work, arrange meetings, schedule vacations, and monitor and evaluate productivity and performance. It also requires that they understand the work-family conflicts their employees face and the policies available to respond to them. Supervisors who focused on structured planning in order to implement flexibility described positive consequences for the entire work group: "The actions we are taking are a little more structured; they are of higher quality; they represent a better employee consideration. It has, in fact, improved the team's overall performance" (Catalyst, 1997, p. 71).

Focus on Effective Communication. Supervisors who manage employees with part-time arrangements successfully emphasize the importance of effective communication about the arrangement with the part-time professional, other members of the work group, and clients. A critical aspect of the conversation supervisors need to have with employees who work part time has to do with the impact of the arrangement on performance evaluation and career advancement. Clear, consistent conversations about performance standards and expectations with everyone involved in the work builds trust and ensures smooth relationships among team members.

Success Strategies for Women Working Part Time. Voluntary part-time arrangements are typically individually negotiated by the employee. Adult education programs, especially those targeted to women, can help women understand and develop the skills critical to negotiating and maintaining successful part-time arrangements and to sustaining a career while working part time temporarily.

Be Informed About Flexible Work Options.   Even if an effective policy exists, there may be few role models or examples within the organization. Negotiating the arrangement requires a clear understanding of (1) the business benefits in order to convince supervisors, (2) an understanding of success factors and best practices in order to evaluate policies and design a successful arrangement, and (3) critical skills and behaviors in order to work part time effectively.

Demonstrate Hard Work, Dedication, and Commitment.   Throughout Catalyst research, women describe their focus on hard work not only in terms of the quality of their work assignments and job, but also in terms of their commitment to making their alternative work schedules successful. A woman explained: "My approach was 'I'm going to work as hard and as well as I can to make this work because it's important to me'" (Catalyst, 1993, p. 38). It is especially important to find ways to maintain a visible presence in the office by communicating plans and schedules, clarifying goals and due dates, and participating in organizational activities. For example, part-time workers can post a sign on their office door, noting their schedules and when they will be in the office. This simple activity can eliminate the comments about part-time people not being around.

Be Flexible and Adaptable.   The most critical characteristic identified for individuals using part-time arrangements is personal flexibility (Catalyst, 1997). This means being willing to accommodate schedules to work demands, handling the typical fluctuations in workload responsibilities, and sometimes remaining accessible and available during nonwork periods. Finding and maintaining flexible child care arrangements is critical.

Formalize and Evaluate the Arrangement.   Successful part-time arrangements are built from explicit discussions about the parameters of the arrangement and work expectations, documented in writing, between the employee and the supervisor (Catalyst, 1993). They also involve regular discussions about the arrangement and how effective it is for both parties. The discussions clarify ways to modify and improve the arrangement.

Prioritize Tasks and Manage Time Effectively.   Women in Catalyst studies who work part time consistently describe the importance of being able to prioritize tasks, learning to be more disciplined, and focusing on meeting goals and productivity. They use their time well.

Build Trusting Relationships.   Professionals with effective part-time arrangements consider building good work relationships with clients, colleagues, and supervisors essential to the success of the relationship (Catalyst, 1997). Investing time in building relationships is critical to building trust. These strong relationships provide opportunities for open discussions about schedules, workload, work expectations, deadlines, and timing for work.

Allow Arrangements to Evolve.   Women with part-time arrangements that last for more than a year describe the importance of allowing the arrangements to evolve to match changes in family responsibilities and schedules, their professional goals, and the work that is available. Evolving work arrangements are described as critical to easing back into full-time work: "It wouldn't have been easy to jump from 25 hours to 40. I increased it to 30 when my daughter started school. Then I started adding a few hours on different weeks when we needed it. . . . So it will be very easy to return to full time work" (Catalyst, 1993, p. 39).

Take Initiative and Have Clear Professional Goals. Those working part time may find that professional opportunities are limited. It is critical for women to be conscious of their own professional goals and to continue to find ways to develop their skills and widen their experiences. These might include lateral opportunities at work or voluntary assignments. Professionals who consider their arrangements successful describe the creative ways they restructure their work, respond to a misconception, or handle a problem (Catalyst, 1997). A part-time client service professional in a consulting firm provided an example: "Last year I had an idea for my performance appraisal. I sent e-mails to my clients and said, 'Performance appraisals are coming up and, if you would like to put in a good word for me with my boss, would you mind e-mailing him?' He was flooded with calls" (Catalyst, 1997, p. 69).

Conclusion

Part-time arrangements can serve as critical tools for women, helping those who feel such arrangements are desirable or necessary to maintain careers during specific life stages that demand major investments of time and attention to personal or family responsibilities. Adult education programs can make a major contribution to women's careers by disseminating information about the arrangements and educating women as employers, supervisors, and employees. Adult education programs targeted to women have a responsibility to expand their curriculums to include the following components:

- Information about the business rationale for adapting traditional schedules as the workforce changes
- Information about part-time work arrangements as an employee option during periods of work and family conflict, including benefits offered and potential impact on career advancement
- Training in the skills that both supervisors and employees using these options need

References

Catalyst. *Flexible Work Arrangements II: Succeeding with Part-time Options.* New York: Catalyst, 1993.

Catalyst. *Making Work Flexible: Policy to Practice.* New York: Catalyst, 1996a.

Catalyst. *Women in Corporate Leadership: Progress and Prospects.* New York: Catalyst, 1996b.

Catalyst. *A New Approach to Flexibility: Managing the Work/Time Equation.* New York: Catalyst, 1997.

Catalyst. *Two Careers, One Marriage: Making It Work in the Workplace.* New York: Catalyst, 1998.

Schneer, J. A., and Reitman, F. "The Interrupted Managerial Career Path: A Longitudinal Study of MBAs." *Journal of Vocational Behavior,* 1997, *51* (3), 411–434.

U.S. Bureau of the Census. *Population Reports.* Washington, D.C.: U.S. Government Printing Office, 1998.

U.S. Bureau of Labor Statistics. *Employment and Earnings.* Washington, D.C.: U.S. Government Printing Office, 1996.

MARCIA BRUMIT KROPF is vice president of research and advisory services at Catalyst, a nonprofit organization that works with business to advance women into leadership.

The role of the human resource development unit is to maximize the potential of all organizational associates. Some initiatives do more to encourage the career progress of women than others.

Human Resource Development's Role in Women's Career Progress

Kimberly S. McDonald, Linda M. Hite

> Sure, women are making progress. But it's not nearly deep or fast enough. . . . Women are jockeying for positions in the middle ranks of organizations, but the top is still a barren plane for them.
>
> Harriet Rubin, 1998, p. 76.

The research confirms the good news and the bad:

- Women represent almost half of the U.S. labor force and hold approximately 43 percent of management positions (U.S. Department of Labor, 1996). However, they continue to comprise only 3 percent of top-level staffs (Catalyst, 1997).
- Despite significant increases in the number of women professionals, job segregation still exists, often resulting in lower-paying positions for women (Snyder, 1994).
- Women are more numerous and visible in organizations than in the past, but the glass ceiling persists, work-family demands continue to present greater hurdles for women than for men, and subtle discrimination still influences women's potential for career advancement. Consequently, organizations' career development opportunities for women have come under greater scrutiny.

Numerous reasons have been cited as deterrents to women's advancement—for example, lack of general management and line experience (Ragins, Townsend, and Mattis, 1998), less exposure to assignments that involve risk and high visibility (Ohlott, Ruderman, and McCauley, 1994), gender discrimination (Cafarella, Clark, and Ingram, 1997; Ragins, Townsend, and Mattis, 1998; Ruderman, Ohlott, and Kram, 1995; Wentling, 1996), difficulty adapting to the corporate culture (Bierema, 1996; Ragins, Townsend, and Mattis, 1998; Wentling, 1996), and lack of a clear career strategy (Wentling, 1996). Much of the research examining women's progress suggests that the human resource development (HRD) function within organizations needs to play an integral role in leveling the playing field.

The Role of HRD

The historic and continuing function of HRD has been to maximize employee potential to contribute to overall organizational strength. This role clearly justifies involvement in women's career progress and interest in the ramifications of inadequate support for women in organizations.

Corporations facing a competitive, global marketplace are recognizing the value of diversity. However, research simultaneously suggests that many senior managers operate under the misconception that their only responsibility is to fill the pipeline with women and wait for results. This assumes that the corporate culture provides equal opportunity to succeed and ignores institutional biases that deter women's advancement beyond middle management (Ragins, Townsend, and Mattis, 1998). Building awareness of the role of the organizational standard-bearers in fostering a more equitable culture is a responsibility that parallels HRD's historical mission of offering training and development programs that strengthen the knowledge, skills, and abilities of corporate associates. This level of awareness building also falls under the purview of HRD in guiding organizational development, since awareness of the issues and an interest in responding to them would lead to systemic change.

As the career and organizational development unit of the corporation, HRD also is best positioned to advocate for women. The dearth of women in upper management positions is a career development issue. Part of the role of HRD is to reexamine the criteria used for selecting candidates for high-potential career tracks, promotions, or succession planning and to check for hidden biases that have been perpetuated by following outdated, although comfortable, practices. From an organizational development perspective, HRD must advocate a more diverse upper management for any corporation hoping to remain competitive in the global market.

Neither awareness nor advocacy will be sufficient, however, if women continue to be denied access to career development opportunities leading to upper management. Women frequently are disregarded, for numerous reasons (double performance standards, stereotypes, biases about women's roles). Regardless of the rationale, the result is the same: women vying for top positions are seen as less prepared, qualified, and experienced, typically because they have not accessed developmental opportunities that build credibility and skills. It is HRD's role to influence access equity, because it is both a career and organizational development issue.

The new era of worldwide competition demands that HRD expand its traditional focus to embrace new responsibilities. Women have made progress in the past two decades, but the glass ceiling remains, and organizations need alternative approaches if they are going to maximize their full workforce potential. HRD, by the nature of its function within organizations, is positioned to lead new initiatives for change, including mentoring, training, career planning, and informal learning.

Mentoring

Mentoring, that is, the connecting of junior staff with senior staff to enhance the career of the former, is a key HRD initiative. Mentoring is discussed at length in Hansman's chapter (this volume) and will be only briefly described here. Mentoring relationships offer not only career guidance and encouragement for the protégés but also opportunities for greater career mobility, insight into organizational culture, and an introduction to the power hierarchy (Fagenson, 1989; Ragins, 1989, 1997; Ragins and Scandura, 1994). This combination of benefits has made mentoring one of the most often cited HRD activities in efforts to break the glass ceiling (Bierema, 1996; Ragins, Townsend, and Mattis, 1998; Wentling, 1996).

However, Ragins and Scandura (1994) also note that women, by not being part of the dominant culture, find establishing such interactions challenging. Barriers to developing informal mentoring relationships range from the tendency of mentors to select protégés most like themselves and the scarcity of upper management women to serve as mentors, to societal taboos about close relationships between males and females (Burke and McKeen, 1990; Cox, 1993; Dreher and Cox, 1996; Hale, 1995). The limited availability of such relationships to women has prompted the development of formal mentoring programs, where a third party, typically the HRD unit, systematically matches mentors and protégés and provides training programs for participants to optimize the benefits for all parties. Although these formal alignments sometimes lack the closeness of mutual selection, they are preferable to the inequities of relying totally on informal choices to determine who has access to this career advantage (Lewis and Fagenson, 1995; Ruderman, Ohlott, and Kram, 1995).

HRD options in implementing a formal mentoring program include group mentoring or mentoring circles, where one mentor or a mentoring pair is assigned to several protégés. Another mentoring alternative, particularly in response to limited mentor availability, is peer mentoring, that is, learning from those at the same level within the organization (Bell, 1996; Kram, 1985).

Finally, women moving up the corporate hierarchy likely will have different types of mentoring needs as their careers progress (Gordon and Whelan, 1998; Kram, 1985). A formalized process, coordinated by HRD, provides the option for assigning successive mentors to fit the developmental needs of protégés. Overall, the HRD function is the natural home for mentoring activities because of its role in career development that yields the maximum good for the organization.

Training

Training opportunities have the potential to influence women's advancement in organizations. A study examining determinants of managerial advancement found that training (which men received more frequently than females) led to promotions (Tharenou, Latimer, and Conroy, 1994). HRD should encourage women to enroll in training programs to gain the knowledge, skills, and abilities needed to advance. HRD can assist women's representation in training programs by making programs available to many levels of employees, examining their training rosters to determine if females are underrepresented in certain types of training programs, and offering training at times and locations that are convenient to many and providing compensation time for participants when seminars, conferences, and meetings require extensive time after hours.

Women's training needs will vary depending on the organization and should be determined through front-end assessments. However, some of the gender research provides guidance regarding training needs. For example, Larwood and Wood (1995), updating a study conducted in 1978, found that women executives wanted additional training in communication and networking and in power and politics. This research suggests that training programs may help women learn about corporate culture and how to be successful within it. The executive women in Bierema's study (1996), however, did not identify training as a major method of learning about organizational culture.

Should HRD create special training programs for women only? Proponents of single-sex training cite the supportive climate and networking opportunities as important reasons for this type of training (Lam, 1990). Opponents suggest that segregating the sexes may result in women feeling more isolated and may invite suggestions that, unlike their male colleagues, women have deficits in key areas.

Lewis and Fagenson (1995) provide this summary for the arguments for and against single-sex training:

> Women-only management training programmes have made significant contributions towards the objective of increased skill. However, the contributions these programmes have made to the objectives of reducing prejudice towards women and increasing the number of women advancing into and being promoted through the ranks of management have been less substantial. Thus, they may not be the ideal strategy to further the development of women in organizations [p. 42].

These authors suggest that "brown-bag" discussion groups and support networks should be considered as "valuable alternatives" to single-sex training events. HRD is well positioned to establish these types of support mechanisms and ensure the availability of training opportunities for all women.

Finally, the literature on gender bias in the college classroom (Gallos, 1993; Maher, 1985; Sadker and Sadker, 1990) and research regarding how women learn (Beer and Darkenwald, 1989; Belenky, Clinchy, Goldberger, and Tarule, 1986; Luttrell, 1989) informs the HRD practitioner that in academic settings, the climate is often perceived as "chilly" for women. In addition Tisdell (1993a, 1993b) suggests that the adult education environment often perpetuates power relationships based on gender, race, class, and age, thus reinforcing the white, male-dominated structure that permeates society. These issues are also likely to be concerns in training. HRD practitioners should scrutinize the training content, methods, classroom interaction patterns, and examples used to determine if the program has the potential to put women in the "outsider" category (Hite and McDonald, 1995).

Career Planning

Career planning, traditionally HRD's charge, has taken on a new dimension as the concept of career path has evolved from progressive steps within an organization to spanning several employers and possibly different areas of expertise. This is an advantage for women, who often have defied the stereotypical career plans put forth by theorists and tradition-bound employers. The linear stages delineated in most career development models have inadequately described women's career paths because their career progression is characterized by change and dividing time between work and family-relationship responsibilities (Caffarella and Olson, 1993). A 1997 study by Caffarella, Clark, and Ingram found that women who chose to follow a linear career path did not have traditional family responsibilities. Most were single, although some cited especially supportive partners or chose to sacrifice marriage for career goals.

HRD is positioned to affect women's career development significantly. Hall (1996) notes that the career of the next century will be "protean," guided by the needs and interests of the individual versus the organization. Schein (1996) adds the dimension of an "internal career" in contrast to the "organizational career." The former is grounded in an individual's "career anchor," a combination of one's talents and abilities, values, and motives or needs regarding career achievement. The entrepreneurial approach to career planning is advocated as well by Gordon and Whelan (1998). They suggest that organizations adopt flexible, broad-based criteria for career success, which would open more opportunities for women who have not followed the traditional career ladder. Together these perspectives acknowledge the value of more individualized and flexible career plans that not only recognize nontraditional career paths but encourage them.

In the light of these decidedly nonlinear career concepts, HRD can educate upper management about alternative routes to career advancement, offer women career planning assistance to optimize their internal career goals, and advocate the legitimacy of the protean career reality. HRD initiatives should include small group training sessions and individual counseling opportunities on structuring one's own career development. Learning sabbaticals, as described by Gordon and Whelan (1998), would provide opportunities to update skills and reassess career goals. Similarly, HRD should advocate selecting more women for high-potential career opportunities and reviewing existing selection criteria for upper-level positions, to check for hidden gender bias.

Women need to feel supported in their quest for advancement. Organizations need to understand the risk of limiting women's career opportunities. HRD can fulfill both of those needs, and it must.

Informal Learning

Informal learning, which occurs through observation and experience, may be most important to women's career development. Women who have climbed the corporate ladder successfully frequently cite the importance of "stretch assignments," taking on risky tasks or positions, and doing consistently outstanding work as factors important in their career progress (Bierema, 1996; Ragins, Townsend, and Mattis, 1998; Wentling, 1996). A Catalyst study (1996) asked executive women to identify company-initiated strategies that were most helpful to their advancement. The women identified high-potential identification and development, high-visibility assignments, and cross-functional job rotations. In the same study, CEOs considered high-visibility assignments to be the most effective strategy for advancing women to senior management.

However, studies also have indicated that many women are not gaining these experiences. For example, women have reported having fewer opportunities to experience certain types of assignments than male peers (Van Velsor and Hughes, 1990). Ohlott, Ruderman, and McCauley (1994) found that women typically held positions and took on assignments that were less visible within their organizations and that involved less risk and less breadth of responsibility than their male counterparts. They write of the dilemma this creates:

> Denying women access to high-level responsibilities creates a vicious cycle in the selection and development process. If women do not have access to these challenges they may be perceived as less qualified than men and may then be unable to qualify for the next job. If a woman's career is later accelerated for affirmative action reasons, the organization may be setting her up for failure because she lacks these experiences [p. 62].

A 1995 study analyzing the promotion decisions of a Fortune 500 company found different reasons given for promotion decisions regarding men and women (Ruderman, Ohlott, and Kram, 1995). Men were more likely to be promoted because they were "known quantities" to their bosses and perceived as being credible to upper management. Managers appeared to be more hesitant to advance women, asking them to prove themselves extensively before promoting them, supposedly to reduce the risk taken by the managers. CEOs point to factors such as women's lack of time in the "pipeline" and lack of line experience as important reasons that many women have not advanced to senior levels within organizations (Ragins, Townsend, and Mattis, 1998).

Clearly, informal learning is a critical career development strategy for women. To counter the glass ceiling, organizations may need to initiate more formal access to developmental activities. HRD can assist in three major ways:

developing cross-functional job rotations, providing diversity training programs for upper management, and serving as an advocate for women.

Catalyst (1996) reports that job rotation programs are uncommon. Yet job rotation could provide women with the experiences they need to realize career goals. HRD could assist by coordinating this program and ensuring that women receive valuable line experience. In some organizations, it may be critical for top management to have overseas experience, yet women are less likely to receive overseas assignments (Antal and Izraeli, 1993). A formalized job rotation program could also help managers obtain this type of experience. A structured program increases the likelihood that women will benefit from job rotations instead of leaving access to such opportunities to chance or favoritism.

HRD may provide diversity training for upper management to raise awareness of gender issues. Specifically, upper management must understand their role in supporting women at all levels. Forty-one percent of CEOs in a 1996 Catalyst study felt that manager accountability for women's advancement was the most effective strategy for advancing women to senior management. However, this same study suggests that senior women and CEOs perceive the corporate environment very differently in terms of women's advancement (Ragins, Townsend, and Mattis, 1998). Training programs emphasizing these discrepancies and providing a forum for men and women to discuss these differences may result in upper management's heightened awareness of barriers that women face and how they can reduce them.

Finally, HRD can advocate for women in organizations. HRD can champion female representation on project teams and task forces, coach women to seek out visible and challenging assignments to develop their technical and managerial abilities, and lobby to increase the representation of women in high-potential candidate groups. Traditionally the informality of "informal learning" has limited women's access to these growth opportunities. HRD's responsibility is to formalize the selection process so that informal learning has access equity.

Conclusion

In the years since the women's movement began, women have made career progress yet generally remain clustered outside the circle of power. Getting women into organizations was the first step, moving them up into management was the second, and selecting women to fill positions of power and influence is the third. Each of the initiatives explored in this chapter has the potential to make a difference, but all have inherent limitations, as Table 6.1 shows. Women's limited access to opportunities seems to be a universal dilemma. Women cannot benefit from an initiative if they cannot gain entry, and the gatekeepers frequently are males. This fact relates to a larger systemic problem. If the organizational culture is not supportive of women's advancement, even the best-structured HRD initiatives will not succeed, because women will not be recognized as viable candidates.

Sometimes the very programs supposedly designed to enhance women's career opportunities actually perpetuate the status quo by teaching women how to survive in an inhospitable culture, how to adapt their styles to fit in, and how to be nonthreatening to the existing power structure. In this instance, even if women are admitted to mentoring, training, career development, and informal learning endeavors, the end result may be no more than that the women who participate are taught to know their place in the organizational hierarchy (that is, be satisfied with less power and opportunity or learn to assimilate and become more like male peers), and the organization smugly celebrates its "openness," as evidenced by all of the programs it has made available to help women adapt to the corporate culture. This is not an acceptable alternative to an inclusive organizational culture.

HRD initiatives have the potential to make a vital contribution to women's career progress. However, they are insufficient mechanisms for change when they are not supported within the organizational culture. Therefore, the role of HRD in fostering women's management development must expand beyond simply providing growth opportunities. HRD's larger purpose must be to influ-

Table 6.1. HRD Initiatives for Enhancing Women's Career Development

Initiative	Opportunities	Concerns	Recommendations
Mentoring	Corporate culture entree Psychosocial support Career guidance Access to power	Limited informal access Formal relationships vary in quality Few mentors available Cross-sex/race issues	Offer group mentoring Advocate peer mentoring Provide training on mentoring skills
Training	Builds professional skills Networking opportunities Enhances self esteem May lead to advancement	Limited access Time limitations and family responsibilities may deter attendance	Ensure access equity Counter common deterrents Offer mixed-sex training
Career Planning	Focuses goals Maximizes skills Clarifies interests Prepares for advancement	Inappropriate career expectations from management Limited access to career guidance Biased high potential selection process	Educate management about flexible career strategies Provide equal access to career guidance Use diverse selection teams to choose high potential candidates
Informal Learning	Multiple options Critical for advancement Chance to prove self	Limited access to opportunities Access to guidance about choices Opportunities involve risk	Use diverse teams to make assignments Promote job rotation programs Encourage management support

ence the culture of the organization, so women are seen as valuable contributors, the playing field really is level, and development of human resources does not mean reinforcing past inequities.

References

Antal, A. B., and Izraeli, D. N. "A Global Comparison of Women in Management: Women Managers in Their Homelands and as Expatriates." In E. A. Fagenson (ed.), *Women in Management.* Thousand Oaks, Calif.: Sage, 1993.

Beer, C. T., and Darkenwald, G. G. "Gender Differences in Adult Student Perceptions of College Classroom Social Environments." *Adult Education Quarterly,* 1989, *40* (1), 33–42.

Belenky, M. F. Clinchy, B. M., Goldberger, N. R., and Tarule, J. M. *Women's Ways of Knowing: The Development of Self, Voice, and Mind.* New York: Basic Books, 1986.

Bell, C. R. *Managers as Mentors: Building Partnerships for Learning.* San Francisco: Berrett-Koehler, 1996.

Bierema, L. "How Executive Women Learn Corporate Culture." *Human Resource Development Quarterly,* 1996, *7* (2), 145–164.

Burke, R. J., and McKeen, C. A. "Mentoring in Organizations: Implications for Women." *Journal of Business Ethics,* 1990, *9,* 317–322.

Caffarella, R. S., Clark, M. C., and Ingram, P. "Life at the Glass Ceiling: Women in Mid-level Management Positions." In P. Armstrong, N. Miller, and M. Zukas (eds.), *Crossing Borders Breaking Boundaries: Research in the Education of Adults.* Proceedings of the 27th Annual SCUTREA (The Standing Committee on University Teaching and Research in the Education of Adults). London, 1997.

Caffarella, R. S., and Olson, S. K. "Psychosocial Development of Women: A Critical Review of the Literature." *Adult Education Quarterly,* 1993, *43* (3), 125–151.

Catalyst. *Women in Corporate Leadership: Progress and Prospects.* New York: Catalyst, 1996.

Catalyst. *1997 Catalyst Census of Women Corporate Officers and Top Earners.* New York: Catalyst, 1997.

Cox, T. H., Jr. *Cultural Diversity in Organizations: Theory, Research and Practice.* San Francisco: Berrett-Koehler, 1993.

Dreher, G. F., and Cox, T. H. "Race, Gender and Opportunity: A Study of Compensation Attainment and the Establishment of Mentoring Relationships." *Journal of Applied Psychology,* 1996, *81* (3), 297–308.

Fagenson, E. A. "The Mentor Advantage: Perceived Career/Job Experiences of Protégés Versus Non-protégés." *Journal of Organizational Behavior,* 1989, *10,* 309–320.

Gallos, J. V. "Women's Experiences and Ways of Knowing: Implications for Teaching and Learning in the Organizational Behavior Classroom." *Journal of Management Education,* 1993, *17* (1), 7–26.

Gordon, J. R., and Whelan, K. S. "Successful Professional Women in Midlife: How Organizations Can More Effectively Understand and Respond to the Challenges." *Academy of Management Executive,* 1998, *12* (1), 8–27.

Hale, M. "Mentoring Women in Organizations: Practice in Search of Theory." *American Review of Public Administration,* 1995, *25* (4), 327–339.

Hall, D. T. "Protean Careers of the 21st Century." *Academy of Management Executive,* 1996, *10* (4), 8–16.

Hite, L. M., and McDonald, K. S. "Gender Issues in Management Development: Implications and Research Agenda." *Journal of Management Development,* 1995, *14* (4), 5–15.

Kaye, B., and Jacobson, B. "Mentoring: A Group Guide." *Training and Development,* 1995, *49* (4), 23–27.

Kram, K. E. *Mentoring at Work: Developmental Relationships in Organizational Life.* Glenview, Ill.: Scott, Foresman, 1985.

Lam, M. N. "Management Training for Women: International Experiences and Lessons for Canada." *Journal of Business Ethics,* 1990, *9,* 385–406.

Larwood, L., and Wood, M. M. "Training Women for Management: Changing Priorities." *Journal of Management Development,* 1995, *14* (2), 54–64.

Lewis, A. E., and Fagenson, E. A. "Strategies for Developing Women Managers: How Well Do They Fulfil Their Objectives?" *Journal of Management Development,* 1995, *14* (2), 39–53.

Luttrell, W. "Working-Class Women's Ways of Knowing: Effects of Gender, Race, and Class." *Sociology of Education,* 1989, *62* (1), 33–46.

Maher, F. "Pedagogies for a Gender-Balanced Classroom." *Feminist Education,* 1985, *20* (3), 48–64.

Ohlott, P. J., Ruderman, M. N., and McCauley, C. D. "Gender Differences in Managers' Developmental Job Experiences." *Academy of Management Journal,* 1994, 37 (1), 46–67.

Ragins, B. R. "Barriers to Mentoring: The Female Manager's Dilemma." *Human Relations,* 1989, *42* (1), 1–22.

Ragins, B. R. "Diversified Mentoring Relationships in Organizations: A Power Perspective." *Academy of Management Review,* 1997, *22* (2), 482–521.

Ragins, B. R., and Scandura, T. A. "Gender Differences in Expected Outcomes of Mentoring Relationships." *Academy of Management Journal,* 1994, 37 (4), 957–971.

Ragins, B. R., Townsend, B., and Mattis, M. "Gender Gap in the Executive Suite: CEOs and Female Executives Report on Breaking the Glass Ceiling." *Academy of Management Executive,* 1998, *12* (1), 28–42.

Rubin, H. "Women and Men, Work and Power." *Fast Company,* Feb./Mar. 1998.

Ruderman, M. N., Ohlott, P .J., and Kram, K. E. "Promotion Decisions as a Diversity Practice." *Journal of Management Development,* 1995, *14* (2), 6–23.

Sadker, M., and Sadker, D. "Confronting Sexism in the College Classroom." In S. L. Gabriel and I. Smithson (eds.), *Gender in the Classroom: Power and Pedagogy.* Urbana: University of Illinois Press, 1990.

Schein, E. H. "Career Anchors Revisited: Implications for Career Development in the 21st Century." *Academy of Management Executive,* 1996, *10* (4), 80–88.

Snyder, N. M. "Career Women in Perspective: The Wichita Sample." In C. W. Konek and S. L. Kitch (eds.), *Women and Careers: Issues and Challenges.* Thousand Oaks, Calif.: Sage, 1994.

Tharenou, P., Latimer, S., and Conroy, D. "How Do You Make It to the Top? An Examination of Influences on Women's and Men's Managerial Advancement." *Academy of Management Journal,* 1994, 37 (4), 899–931.

Tisdell, E. J. "Feminism and Adult Learning: Power, Pedagogy, and Praxis." In S. Merriam (ed.), *An Update on Adult Learning Theory.* New Directions for Adult and Continuing Education, no. 57. San Francisco: Jossey-Bass, 1993a.

Tisdell, E. J. "Interlocking Systems of Power, Privilege, and Oppression in Adult Higher Education Classes." *Adult Education Quarterly,* 1993b, *43* (4), 203–226.

U.S. Department of Labor. "Employed Persons by Occupation, Race, and Sex." *Employment and Earnings.* Washington, D.C.: Department of Labor, 1996.

Van Velsor, E., and Hughes, M. W. *Gender Differences in the Development of Managers: How Women Managers Learn from Experience.* Greensboro, N.C.: Center for Creative Leadership, 1990.

Wentling, R. M. "A Study of the Career Development and Aspirations of Women in Middle Management." *Human Resource Development Quarterly,* 1996, 7 (3), 253–270.

KIMBERLY S. MCDONALD *is program coordinator and associate professor of organizational leadership and supervision at Indiana University–Purdue University Fort Wayne, Fort Wayne, Indiana.*

LINDA M. HITE *is associate professor in organizational leadership and supervision at Indiana University–Purdue University Fort Wayne, Fort Wayne, Indiana.*

Mentoring relationships have the potential to enhance women's career development. However, women encounter challenges while forging cross-gender and same-gender mentoring relationships.

Mentoring and Women's Career Development

Catherine A. Hansman

Many mentors have assisted me along various career paths. One was an older chain-smoking male colleague who dropped pieces of advice along with cigarette ashes on my desk in my early career as a computer analyst for the Air Force. One of the few women with whom I worked also took interest in my career and mentored me through thorny job issues. As my career path changed over the years, other mentors stepped forward in both employer-designed mentoring programs and informal mentoring relationships.

A woman's career development, as mine has, may be enhanced or even depend on the helpful relationships formed with more experienced colleagues. Mentoring relationships have been shown to affect protégés' careers positively and are related to achievement and influence in organizations, which leads to protégés' earning higher salaries (Dreher and Cox, 1996; Fagenson 1989; Turban and Doughtery, 1994; Whitely, Doughtery and Dreher, 1988). Having a mentor may help increase the quality of organizational life for women and may help alleviate stress by increasing self-esteem (Nelson and Quick, 1985). Further, protégés in mentoring relationships with senior employees may gain special forms of entry into meaningful social networks and acquire important managerial skills by observing effective senior management (Dreher and Ash, 1990). However, research on mentoring relationships has shown that these relationships are frequently less available to women than to men (Cox, 1993; Hansman and Garofolo, 1995; Hill, Bahniuk, and Dobos, 1989; Hite, 1998). Moreover, initiating mentoring relationships can be problematic and complex for women, particularly when all potential mentors are male. Some of the barriers women face are lack of women mentors (Hunt and Michael, 1983; Collard and Stalker, 1991), problems with men mentoring women (Burke,

McKeen and McKenna, 1990; Stalker, 1994), and conflicts between work and family responsibilities (Vertz, 1985; Blunt and Lee, 1994).

Four barriers for women seeking mentoring stand out in the literature. First, because organizations continue to be dominated by white males, women have difficulty initiating and maintaining mentor-protégé relationships. Second, even with mentors, women may experience more problems meeting their career goals than men do. Third, cross-gender mentoring creates unique concerns for which little research exists (Hale, 1995). Finally, the concept of mentoring itself and how it may perpetuate hegemonic cultural structures within organizations needs further examination.

Defining Mentoring

Contemporary definitions of *mentoring* vary, although most capture elements of nurturing and guiding characteristics. Daloz (1986) asserts that mentors are essentially guides who "lead us along the journey of our lives. They embody our hopes, cast light on the way ahead, interpret arcane signs, warn us of lurking dangers, and point out unexpected delights along the way" (p. 17). Caffarella (1992) takes a more career-oriented view of mentors by explaining that mentoring involves "an intense caring relationship in which persons with more experience work with less experienced persons to promote both professional and personal development" (p. 38).

Psychosocial and Career Mentors. The quality of mentoring relationships seems to depend on the roles mentors play with their protégés. Kram (1983) identifies psychosocial and career-related functions of mentoring. Psychosocial mentors enhance protégés' esteem and confidence and are dependent on interpersonal dynamics and emotional bonds. Some studies suggest that women are more comfortable within psychosocial mentoring relationships (Kram and Isabella, 1985; Noe, 1988). Career-related mentors may also increase self-esteem and confidence, but these mentors may be more likely to sponsor protégés, introduce them to the "right" people, protect protégés from organizational climate, and help protégés prepare for advancement and obtain promotions. Career-related mentors are more likely to help protégés develop marketable skills, behaviors, and attitudes related to the workplace.

It is important for women to be involved in both informal and formal mentoring relationships. Informal mentoring happens through mutual discovery of common interests and relationship building. Formal mentoring is generally organization sponsored and focused on recruitment, retention, succession planning, and organizational change efforts.

Peer Mentors. If establishing mentoring relationships with senior employees is difficult, Kram (1985) and Noe (1988) point out that peer mentoring relationships may be an important alternative for women. Kram and Isabella (1985) conclude that peer relationships provide developmental support for personal and professional growth. They describe three types of peer relationships: informational peers, who provide each other with beneficial information; collegial peers, who are like informational peers but exchange higher levels of trust and self-disclosure that leads to more emotional support; and special peers, who are the "equivalent of best friends" (Kram and Isabella, 1988, p. 120) and provide the widest range of career and psychosocial support.

Riley and Wrench (1985) found that women professionals may have a number of supportive relationships that they refer to as group mentoring. For example, a study of women doctoral students who were not in mentoring relationships with faculty members found that they formed supportive groups with other graduate students for professional encouragement and affirmation (Hansman and Garofolo, 1995). Besides workplace peers, outside friends and even family members may be a source of peer or group mentoring, particularly since friends or relatives are not competing within the same organization or profession and may have a more holistic understanding of the protégé as a person (McKeen and Burke, 1989).

Because women may be comfortable with psychosocial mentoring relationships, they may not seek career-related mentors who might be more helpful in career advancement. Women engaged only in peer mentoring relationships should examine their effectiveness in enhancing career development. Table 7.1 looks at the benefits of these peer relationships.

Table 7.1. Benefits of Mentoring Relationships

Type of Mentoring	Benefits of Mentoring Relationship
Career-related Mentoring	Sponsor protégé Protect protégé from organizational politics Introduce protégé to "right" people Provide career advice Help advance protégé's career Enhance protégé's esteem and confidence Typically mentor is a supervisor or someone with more experience within the organization or field, same or opposite gender
Psychosocial Mentoring	Interpersonal relationship Friendship and emotional support important Role model for protégé Enhance protégé's esteem and confidence Help advance protégé's career Typically mentor is a supervisor or someone with more experience within the organization or field, same or opposite gender
Peer Mentoring	Support for both personal and professional development Friendship and emotional support essential Career advancement possible, but not always only goal of the relationship Trading information for career growth High levels of trust and collegiality Typically mentor is on the same level as protégé; more likely to be a relationship among equals, friends or even family members

Women's Challenges: Facing the Real World of Mentoring in the Workplace

While formal mentoring relationships may help women's career advancement, problems associated with both formal and informal mentoring programs remain. For example, finding mentors in male-dominated workplaces may be difficult for women. Male mentors may be assigned to women protégés; however, when compared to female mentors, they provide much less career development and psychosocial functions, such as career planning, performance feedback, and personal support (Burke, McKean, and McKenna, 1990). There may be few women role models in organizations, or successful women who have fought for their places within their organizations may not be willing to mentor junior women. Women's choices concerning marriage, childbearing, and careers (or assumptions by males and others about these choices) may lead to perceptions that women are less committed to their careers, thus limiting their participation in mentoring relationships. Women of color face difficult challenges in organizations as the intersection of gender and race plays out in the workplace and in their careers.

Cross-Gender Mentoring. In Homer's *Odyssey,* Athena became a man to mentor Telemachus, thus creating the largely androcentric view of mentoring that prevails. Much of the early research on mentoring assumes that the gender of either the mentor or the protégé does not affect how the relationships are formed or the quality of the interactions between mentor and protégé (Stalker, 1994; Merriam, 1983). However, Kram (1985) identified five major cross-gender mentoring relationship complexities: collusion in stereotypical roles, limitations of role modeling, intimacy and sexuality concerns, public scrutiny, and peer resentment.

Collusion in stereotypical roles presents a problem when men and women assume stereotypical roles in relating to each other in work settings, such as father–daughter, chivalrous knight–helpless maiden, tough warrior–weak warrior, and macho–seductress (Feist-Price, 1994). *Role model mentoring* involves both interaction and identification with someone else of higher stature. When professional and personal concerns of mentors and protégés are different in a mentoring relationship, problems with interaction may occur. Because many women face problems between work and family commitments, particularly if they are one of few women in a male-dominated workplace, identifying with male role models may become difficult or impossible.

Because men may prefer interacting with and mentoring males whom they perceive to be more like themselves (Dreher and Cox, 1996), they may choose to develop protégé relationships with other men (McKeen and Burke, 1989) and exclude women colleagues as protégés. Concerns about public image may also cause male mentors to avoid establishing mentoring relationships with women. *Intimacy and sexuality tensions* may be a source of anxiety for both males and females who do participate in cross-gender mentoring relationships. Mentors and protégés who work together to develop their careers require some level of intimacy and close relationship. With heightened concerns about sexual harassment, men may avoid mentoring women or may behave more remotely toward them than toward other men to avoid the possibility or appearance of an intimate relationship. As a result, the cross-gender mentoring relationship may become useless to women protégés.

Public scrutiny of the cross-gender mentoring relationship may also limit its development. For example, in same-gender mentoring relationships, mentor and protégé may meet outside work for social activities that would cause no discussion of appropriateness of these actions in the workplace. However, in cross-gender mentoring situations, if men and women participate together in after-work social activities, they may become the targets of rumors and damaging gossip about sexual involvement. Public perception may thus limit men (and women's) willingness to participate in mentoring relationships. Women may then lack access to important information networks and resources that will further their careers. In addition, peers who perceive that women protégés within the organization are receiving special help from powerful men mentors may resent the women and throw stumbling blocks in their career paths.

Women Mentoring Women. If cross-gender mentoring poses problems, it seems logical that same-gender mentoring relationships would be more beneficial. However, although same-gender mentor-protégé relationships may be advantageous, issues still remain that affect the efficacy of these relationships. First, a major problem for women seeking women to mentor them is the limited number of women in leadership or higher management positions. Potential women mentors may be overwhelmed and have other pressures limiting their availability to protégés. Protégés may also complicate matters by establishing unrealistic expectations of mentors that demand more time and emotional energy than women mentors are willing or able to give (Eldridge, 1990). Second, although Burke, McKeen, and McKenna (1990) reported that psychosocial functions were significantly more common in same-gender female relationships, these functions may not provide the best type of career help that is valued in the workplace. The psychosocial functions of friendship and social support are not always what propel women ahead in organizations. Finally, women may be seen by both male and female colleagues as having less power, and thus less influence as mentors, in the workplace (Hale, 1995).

Family Demands. Potential barriers to women's career development and participation in mentoring relationship include family and child care responsibilities. Women who are delaying or interrupting their careers for childbearing often experience late career entries or career interruptions, which could lead to difficulties in forming and maintaining mentoring relationships (Chandler, 1996). This means that potential mentors, both male and female, may focus their efforts on men protégés instead of women because they perceive men as being "more serious" about their careers (Chandler, 1996).

Women of Color and Mentoring. Women of color face the same issues concerning mentoring as do European American women, and their challenges are compounded by the intersection of race and gender. Not much research has focused on women of color and mentoring relationships in organizations (Hite, 1998). Ramey (1993) found that having a mentor is very important for women of color in higher education administrative careers. Another study concluded that support networks were essential for the success of women minority students in hostile academic environments (Morgan, 1993). Since "women of color are twice removed from the ranks of dominant culture, based on their race as well as gender, their potential need for the benefits of mentoring would appear to be even greater than that of their white female colleagues" (Hite, 1998, p. 786). Hite's (1998) study of black female professionals shows that these women did experience mentoring; however, respondents to her survey indicated the need for increased availability of same-sex and same-race mentors.

Chandler (1996) argues that women of historically marginalized groups may have different needs and expectations than nonminority women have and that research concerning mentoring and women should expand beyond the white middle-class model. In support of this idea, Guinier, Fine, and Balin (1997) take issue with the idea that protégés must find someone of their own gender or ethnic group to serve as models. They suggest that both European American women and women of color in role model positions be examined and honored for the contributions they make in diversifying their organizations and showing how traditional roles may be performed differently, not just be viewed as "token" examples of achievement. Their book's telling title, *Becoming Gentlemen,* raises an important question of whether all women of any race must adopt and conform to male models of achievement to be successful.

Mentoring as Sanctioning Elitist Behavior. Carden (1990) questions contemporary notions of mentoring, asking whether mentoring "sanctions an elitist patron system that excludes the socially different . . . and maintains a status quo based on accumulation of advantage and replication of exploitive hierarchical systems" (p. 276). Stalker (1994), in her critique of mentoring in academe, states that traditional research and models of mentoring are androcentric. Furthermore, she contends that problems inherent in men mentoring women are not discussed in the literature of adult education, and assumptions are made that women mentors will reproduce the "patriarchal academe" (p. 365) that is dominant in universities.

These ideas lead to important questions about mentoring in organizations for which there are no easy answers. Do women in positions of power become cocreators with members of the dominant culture of workplaces and continue creating the experiences of "isolation and invisibility" (Stalker, 1994) for junior women that they have experienced themselves? How can women contribute to organizations yet not become part of a hegemonic culture that keeps those of different gender, ethnicity, race, or sexual orientation from fully participating? And finally, do mentoring relationships simply reproduce existing power structures within organizations, or can they allow women to contribute to truly diversifying organizations through recognizing the contributions women make?

Conclusion

There are no easy answers to any of these questions. Clearly mentoring relationships have the potential for enhancing women's career development, and organizations that acknowledge this possibility are creating formal mentoring programs designed to reach women and minorities.

When designing formal workplace mentoring programs, organizations should clearly communicate the goals of the program (organizational goals versus employee developmental goals), criteria for participation, and guidelines for interaction between mentors and protégés. Women who participate in these programs should make sure they understand the possible gains and potential pitfalls of participating. Meetings that inform participants about the program may also serve to boost communication between mentor and protégé. More research is needed concerning the successes that formal mentoring programs have achieved in promoting women within organizations.

However helpful they may be, formal mentoring programs are not a cure-all for women's career development. Women may still need to seek other informal mentoring relationships to strengthen their career and personal achievements. Organizations should view contributions to the workplace culture from women and minority employees as valid additions to defining roles within the workplace. Mentoring relationships that allow women and minorities to not only conform but contribute to workplace cultures will further women's careers. Finally, organizations that promote, respect, and value achievements of women and historically marginalized groups will add to women's progress in the workplace.

References

Blunt, A., and Lee, J. "The Contribution of Graduate Student Research to Adult Education/*Adult Education Quarterly,* 1969–1988." *Adult Education Quarterly,* (1994), *44* (3), 125–144.

Burke, R. J., McKeen, C. A., and McKenna, C. S. "Sex Differences and Cross-Sex Effects on Mentoring: Some Preliminary Data." *Psychological Reports,* 1990, *67,* 1011–1028.

Caffarella, R. S. *Psychosocial Development of Women.* Information Series, no. 350. Columbus, Ohio: ERIC Clearinghouse on Adult, Career and Vocational Education, 1992.

Carden, A. D. "Mentoring and Adult Career Development." *Counseling Psychologist,* 1990, *18* (2), 275–299.

Chandler, C. "Mentoring and Women in Academia: Reevaluating the Traditional Model." *NWSA Journal,* 1996, 8 (3), 79–100.

Collard, S., and Stalker, J. "Women's Trouble." In R. Hiemstra (ed.), *Creating Environments for Effective Adult Learning.* New Directions in Adult and Continuing Education, no. 50. San Francisco: Jossey-Bass, 1991.

Cox, T. H. *Cultural Diversity in Organizations: Theory, Research and Practice.* San Francisco: Berrett-Koehler, 1993.

Daloz, L. *Effective Teaching and Mentoring: Realizing the Transformational Power of Adult Learning Experiences.* San Francisco: Jossey-Bass, 1986.

Dreher, G. F., and Ash, R. A. "A Comparative Study of Mentoring Among Men and Women in Managerial, Professional, and Technical Positions." *Journal of Applied Psychology,* 1990, *75* (5), 539–546.

Dreher, G. F., and Cox, T. H. "Race, Gender and Opportunity: A Study of Compensation Attainment and the Establishment of Mentoring Relationships." *Journal of Applied Psychology*, 1996, *81* (3), 297–308.

Eldridge, N. S. "Mentoring from the Self-In Relation Perspective." Paper presented to the Annual Convention of the American Psychological Association, Boston, 1990. (ED 24548)

Fagenson, E. A. "The Mentor Advantage: Perceived Career/Job Experiences of Protégés vs. Non-Protégés." *Journal of Organizational Behavior*, 1989, *10*, 309–320.

Feist-Price, S. "Cross-Gender Mentoring Relationships: Critical Issues." *Journal of Rehabilitation*, Apr.–June 1994, pp. 13–17.

Guinier, L., Fine, M., and Balin, J. *Becoming Gentlemen: Women, Law School, and Institutional Change.* Boston: Beacon Press, 1997.

Hale, M. H. "Mentoring Women in Organization: Practice in Search of Theory." *American Review of Public Administration*, 1995, *25* (4), 327–339.

Hansman, C., and Garofolo, P. "Toward a Level Playing Field: The Roles of Mentors and Critical Friendships in the Lives of Women Doctoral Students." In *Proceedings of the 34th Annual Adult Education Research Conference, 1985.* Alberta, Canada: University of Alberta, 1995.

Hill, S. E. K., Bahniuk, M. H., and Dobos, J. "Mentoring and Other Communication Support Systems in the Academic Setting." *Group and Organizational Studies*, 1989, *14*, 355–368.

Hite, L. "Race, Gender and Mentoring Patterns." In *1998 Proceedings of the Academy of Human Resource Development Conference.* Oak Brook, Ill., 1998.

Hunt, D. M., and Michael, C. "Mentorship." *Academy of Management Review*, 1983, *8*, 475–484.

Kram, K. "Phases of the Mentor Relationship." *Academy of Management Journal*, 1983, *26*, 608–625.

Kram, K. *Mentoring at Work: Developmental Relationships in Organizational Life.* Glenview, Ill.: Scott, Foresman, 1985.

Kram, K., and Isabella, L. A. "Mentoring Alternatives: The Role of Peer Relationships in Career Development." *Academy of Management Journal*, 1985, *28* (1), 110–128.

Loeb, M. "The New Mentoring." *Fortune*, 1995, *132* (11), 213.

McKeen, C. A., and Burke, R. J. "Mentor Relationship in Organizations: Issues, Strategies and Prospects for Women." *Journal of Management Development*, 1989, *8* (3), 33–42.

Merriam, S. "Mentors and Protégés: A Critical Review of Literature." *Adult Education Quarterly*, 1983, *33* (3) 161–173.

Morgan, J. "Women Leaders of Color Call for Coalition and Unity to Advance Concerns." *Black Issues in Higher Education*, 1993, *10*, 4, 22–23.

Nelson, D. L., and Quick, J. D. "Professional Women: Are Distress and Disease Inevitable?" *Academy of Management Review*, 1985, *10*, 206–218.

Noe, R. A. "Women and Mentoring. A Review and Research Agenda." *Academy of Management Review*, 1988, *13*, 65–78.

Ramey, F. H. "Mentoring: Its Role in the Advancement of Women Administrators in Higher Education." *Black Issues in Higher Education*, 1993, *10* (17), 116.

Redmond, S. P. "Mentoring and Cultural Diversity in Academic Settings." *American Behavioral Scientist*, 1990, *34* (2), 210–222.

Riley, S., and Wrench, D. "Mentoring Among Women Lawyers." *Journal of Applied Social Psychology*, 1985, *15* (4), 374–386.

Stalker, J. "Athene in Academe: Women Mentoring Women in the Academy." *International Journal of Lifelong Education*, 1994, *13* (5), 361–372.

Turban, D. B., and Doughtery, T. W. "Role of Protégé Personality in Receipt of Mentoring and Career Success." *Academy of Management Journal*, 1994, *3* (3), 688–702.

Vertz, L. L. "Women, Occupational Advancement, and Mentoring: An Analysis of One Public Organization." *Public Management Forum*, May–June 1985, pp. 415–423.

Whitely, W., Doughtery, T. W., and Dreher, G. F. "The Relationship of Mentoring and Socioeconomic Origin to Managers' and Professionals' Early Career Progress." *Academy of Management Best Paper Proceedings*, 1988, 58–62.

CATHERINE A. HANSMAN is assistant professor of adult education in the Department of Counseling, Administration, Supervision, and Adult Learning, Cleveland State University, Cleveland, Ohio.

The education of trade union women, besides bread-and-butter trade union courses, needs to include a holistic approach to address their dual roles as caretakers and workers.

Women's Career Development in Trade Unions: The Need for a Holistic Approach

M. Catherine Lundy

The changes in the U.S. workforce have brought with them the erosion of trade union membership and an increase in working women. The paradox of this situation is that most of the current literature on unions expresses a growing interest among women in joining trade unions. Women's interest has not gone unnoticed, and trade unions now view women as a viable source of increasing membership. Women are interested in trade unions because they are potential sources of increased earning power. The Institute for Women's Policy Research (1994) reports that women covered under a collective bargaining agreement have higher wages and longer job tenure. They also enjoy a smaller pay gap between men and women. The question remains, Why are unions struggling for members when nearly 50 percent of the workforce is female? What obstacles prevent women from fully embracing trade unions? Why are women excluded from leadership positions? Can one assume that the perception of trade unions as male-dominated bastions of power and prestige still exists? If this is the case, what can trade unions do to make themselves more attractive and receptive to females?

Growth of Female-Majority Labor Unions

Since the 1960s and 1970s unions have grown in the female-dominated sectors of the economy: education; federal, state, and municipal governments; and the health care industry. Consequently, as of 1990, labor unions constituted a majority of women members in the newer international unions, which

NEW DIRECTIONS FOR ADULT AND CONTINUING EDUCATION, no. 80, Winter 1998 © Jossey-Bass Publishers emerged in the 1960s: the American Federation of State, County and Municipal Employees (AFSCME), the Service Employees International Union (SEIU), the National Education Association (NEA), and the American Nurses Association (ANA). Women also dominate in older internationals, such as the United Food and Commercial Workers (UFCW) and the Communications Workers of America (CWA). And many of the most powerful and vocal internationals within the labor movement are now unions with large female constituents. These unions have provided national leadership on a wide range of women's concerns, from pay equity to parental leave. Cobble (1993) believes that this growth of female-dominated unions will alter the gender composition of organized labor and lead to a more women-responsive labor movement.

Female interest in unions is expected to continue, according to Kruse and Schur (1992). Their research indicates that 40 percent of women would vote for a union if given the chance as compared to only 35 percent for all nonunion workers. Furthermore, organizing survey data (AFL-CIO, 1988) revealed that unions won 57 percent of all campaigns conducted in female-dominated workplaces (units with 75 percent or more women), as compared to 33 percent with a majority of men. Even with this interest shown by women and the potential to increase trade union membership, the number of females in leadership positions is not proportionate to their numbers in trade union membership. Why this is the case may be based on how unions operate and how this adversely affects female leadership positions.

Women as Union Leaders

That union officials are elected positions presents a significant barrier when women attempt to climb the union ladder. This is evident in the fact that women are not achieving the desirable representation in union leadership positions. The male-dominated union culture remains strong, for traditions die hard, and underrepresentation in women's leadership positions remains a problem. Of the eighty-nine national unions affiliated with the AFL-CIO, only three have a female president, and the others account for only 9 percent of top elected positions. Women, however, fare better in national union appointed or staff positions, where one-third of them are employed. Unfortunately, administrative positions carry little power when compared to elected posts (Koziara and Pierson, 1980).

Research reported by Cobble (1993) on female membership and leadership in selected labor organizations from 1978 to 1990 demonstrates that in all unions, the female percentage of members is not reflected in the percentage of top leadership positions (officers and board members). Unions therefore still tend to be male dominated. Women are making process, although it is very slow. Their numbers in leadership positions are increasing at the union local level. More recent research shows that women are now holding more elected offices in local unions (Baden, 1986; Goldberg, 1995), although the typical top officer in a local union is a forty-six-year-old married white male with a high school education.

Research of 298 locals indicates that percentages of top local women offi-cers are at nearly 10 percent. These women have been holding these offices in recently established service sector locals for a mean of 6.9 years. Further, a gen-eral trend is for women to serve as first-line stewards or sit on committees that hold no real power. The majority of these women continue to face educational and informational barriers as they move up the ladder at the local level, and their lack of union skills tends to shut them out of the power structure. These barriers, in turn, affect the proportions of women who are running for and attaining national office (Chaison and Andiappan, 1989).

Reasons for the lack of informational and educational opportunities for women are that women are clustered in positions of low rank and little power, so they are the least likely candidates to be sent to educational conferences or training workshops. And because they have not developed the requisite skills, their opportunities for upward mobility are limited. Elkiss (1994) suggests that the key reason women are facing these issues is the glass ceiling that exists for women who attempt to move into top leadership positions in their unions, the same glass ceiling in corporate America that effectively blocks qualified women from positions of executive power.

Female Barriers to Obtaining Leadership Positions

Dipoye (1987) discusses women's problems and progress in management and suggests that there are four levels that explain women's underrepresentation and slow progress up corporate ladders; these can be applied as well to union women:

1. The individual level, which suggests that the problem stems from women's deficiencies in knowledge, skill, and personality, as well as male and female attitudinal barriers
2. The interpersonal level, which suggests that men and women adopt social roles inconsistent with the integration of women into a traditionally male domain
3. The group level, which suggests that men tend to exclude women from the informal networks that are crucial to acquiring power and influence within the organization
4. The culture and environment, which block women's upward mobility

Women in management positions still face barriers to career advancement, such as biases in the perceptions and evaluations of their performance in super-visory roles, greater conflicts between work and family, sexual harassment, lack of mentors, bias in job assignments, fewer networking opportunities, and stereo-typing of women's roles. These same barriers prevail for union women. In addi-tion, "In sharp contrast to other professions, the careers of union leaders are rarely planned. Becoming a leader in a union tends to be an accidental vocational choice that grows out of complex patterns of experiences and relationships in the trade or occupation in which one is employed" (Gray, 1993, p. 381). This accidental character and political dynamic of the personnel selection process in unions sheds light on why so few women have emerged as top leaders, a pattern that has an adverse impact on all female union members.

Delaney and Lundy (1997) found that when females are neither vocal about their issues nor present during discussions around issues, such as during collective bargaining sessions, their issues tend to go unmet. For example, during contract negotiations, male bargaining teams may be more inclined than female bargaining teams to drop a child care proposal. Eaton (1992) reports that this tendency to ignore women's issues still exists, even though women trade unionists have organized and argued for a rightful place in the labor movement for years. Women need to be present at the bargaining table, and to get there they need training that will give them the necessary skills and education to run for and hold union elected officer positions. For women to be properly trained, one needs to look in general at the whole area of adult education and specifically where labor education fits in. This also holds true for human resource development (HRD), labor education's counterpart, which has experienced a similar problem.

HRD and Labor Education

Dirkx (1996) has observed that work-related education and training in HRD occupies "a curious intellectual space in the broader landscape of adult learning with adult educators disagreeing as to whether it should be considered a part of their field" (p. 41). The dispute centers on adult education's philosophy that includes social justice, lifelong learning, and the empowerment of people. HRD's philosophy tends to be narrower, focusing on the corporate bottom line favoring the organization's needs over employees' needs. Corporate management needs typically drive HRD's goals and objectives. Bierema (1996) concludes that it would be advantageous to combine both approaches and offer holistic development that integrates personal and professional life in career planning and gives adults the opportunity and incentive to learn.

Trade union education could benefit from the holistic advice, especially since trade union philosophy centers on social justice and the empowerment of workers. By the nature of this belief, it should be important for unions not to abandon long-term objectives in pursuit of short-term organizational goals. Yet this is not the case, according to Brickner (1976), who stated that traditional labor education, interdisciplinary in its subject matter and teaching methods, is driven by the changing demands of unions. This approach is limiting in the sense that most officers will place the focus of labor education on their need to meet their administrative work objectives and not the individual union member's objectives.

Both approaches, labor education and HRD, are self-limiting and narrow. Although this commonality exists between them, there is a vital difference: unions are voluntary organizations. HRD can require employees to attend workshops and seminars; unions cannot. For unions, the need for strategic decision making toward labor education is vital. Women members not only need to be encouraged to join and participate in the union, but also need organizational support to develop into leaders who can act as a voice for the issues and concerns of women.

Training and Women

Training is the key strategy for individual women, and most women leaders have learned their skills through a combination of formal and informal (on-the-job) training and mentoring (Eaton, 1992). They have taken courses on conducting local meetings, presenting motions, running for office, public speaking, collective bargaining, union structure, labor law, and employment law. These educational measures are inevitably linked to the resources and institutional support that the organization gives them (Trebilcock, 1991). When projects are funded and focus on union rank and file women, the results can be impressive. Unions have experimented with many different approaches to train their members.

One evaluated program was the Leadership Training Project, which demonstrated that when unions support educational training, female union members develop leadership skills. The Leadership Training Project for women and minorities was founded in 1979 by the Michigan State University Labor Education Department (LEP, 1991). The program lasted until 1993, when funding was eliminated by line-item cuts by the Michigan State legislature. The program coordinator was Eula Booker Tate, who came from the rank and file of the UAW as a truck driver. She earned her degree at the University of Michigan and was hired as the program administrator. Booker's background lent understanding to the need for rank-and-file women to have training programs that gave them the opportunity to network and learn union and leadership skills in a safe and supportive environment.

Each year this project held a three-day conference, Michigan State Winter School for Women Worker, attended by rank-and-file union women from throughout Michigan. Attendees to the conference enlisted their unions for funds to attend the conference. Consequently the majority of registrants were sponsored and paid for by union funds. Some others were eligible for scholarships. Usually about two hundred union women and three men attended. Conference development was constructed through a series of planning meetings with union women to develop the agendas and plan the event. At the conference, union women introduced speakers and eventually became the presenters.

A survey of the program was conducted in 1989 to evaluate how respondents viewed themselves in 1979 and how they viewed themselves in 1989 after regular attendance at Leadership Training Project classes. A measure was taken to qualify the change in behavior caused by the participation in one or several of the leadership training programs. The results showed that students viewed themselves as more aggressive, more active in clubs or groups and group affairs, more confident in performing their duties, and better able to take risks; moreover, the number of women in leadership positions had doubled. These results were a significant indication that leadership skills taught at the program influenced the participants' ability and desire to be leaders. Thus, the program affected the participants' upward mobility in a positive manner. (Besides this project are many different programs provided by trade unions and colleges and universities in the United States that are involved in labor education.)

Labor educators have their own professional association that measures success or failures in their field. The University and College Labor Education Association (UCLEA) has sixty-nine institutional member council affiliates, which include most of the major higher education institutions. The purpose of UCLEA is to provide recognized programs in the field of labor education and labor studies that serve workers and their organizations. The programmatic styles vary. Some are linked to academic centers that provide credit courses, others operate on a noncredit basis, and some offer both options.

Annually the UCLEA and the American Federation of Labor–Congress of Industrial Unions (AFL-CIO) hold a joint conference with the purpose bringing labor educators together to discuss issues and present educational workshops on topics of vital concern. Even with this coordinated effort, the issue of women's lack of proportional leadership positions in unions still exists.

Why Are Union Women Still at the Bottom of the Ladder?

Cook (1992) indicates that even when urged to apply for educational programs, many women hesitate because home and work pressures outweigh the benefits they perceive. Union participation and education take time and sacrifice, and many women are simply not able to join in. It has been said that "labor education in unions and universities has a long tradition of experiential, action-oriented education for union activists" (Gray, 1976, p. 41), but it has missed the mark when it comes to union women's career development. If union women have not been successful in breaking through the glass ceiling in their unions, who is to blame? Is it that unions and labor education centers have not listened to and provided for the needs of union women to develop career paths? Or is it that society discriminates against them and expects their role to be limited to the home? Maybe it is both, and what needs to be addressed is a new system for women—a plan that will incorporate women's lifestyles, their workplace, and their union into a holistic approach for career path development.

What Unions and University Labor Education Centers Can Do to Assist Women's Career Path Development

Unless they are without family obligations, women cannot afford a tremendous amount of time for themselves. We live in a society where women are generally expected to pick up the cost to society for any duties considered "women's work." For example, when home health care or generic care becomes too expensive for paid help, it will shift back to women to be performed as unpaid work (Glazer, 1993). This adds to women's burdens and decreases their free time even further. Women have told me that they could not participate in a union drive or a negotiation session because their husband would not allow them to take the time away from the home. Is it possible that everything that is being done is all that is possible in the way of education for union women? What could help them to succeed in their unions? Women do not have time to waste in either their career or home lives. They need to be afforded a system that gives them credit for their life experiences and supports them with their child care and home care responsibilities. This means that in order to succeed, women need a holistic approach to career path development.

As Gleason has said, "There is no one road to freedom. There are roads to freedom" (1921, p. 22). Women need to have more roads open for them—for example, seminars, workshops, and conferences. And attendance needs to mean something more than just giving up some time. It needs to be applied toward some long-term objective, as in credit toward a degree or continuing education credits.

Credits Toward a Degree. Labor unions or labor education centers could contract with community colleges or other centers of higher education to provide credit for their educational classes. This may mean that some sort of testing arrangement will need to be developed, but this method has been used, although somewhat differently, when adults test for lifelong credit at four-year institutions.

Continuing Education Credits. Unions and labor education centers should, whenever applicable, provide continuing education credits (CEUs) for their participants. For example, Michigan State University and the University of Illinois Labor Education Programs hold an annual conference for labor representatives in the health care industry, among them, nurses. Nursing now requires CEUs in order to maintain licensure, and labor education provides continuing credit by filing applications with state nursing associations, thus enabling conference participants to receive credit for their attendance.

Internet Union Training Programs. Trade unions and labor education centers could provide classes on the Internet in order to reach a wide audience. Internet classes are being offered through various institutions even now, and these resources are available to unions and labor education centers. Computers could be made available through the union hall, higher education centers, or some other means, such as rental for women who do not own their own computer.

Child Care Arrangements. Most of these innovative arrangements will fail if women are unable to leave their home to participate in the programs because of child care issues. Labor unions and labor education centers will have to look seriously at alternative ways to deal with this issue. There may be some way to trade off child care obligations with other union members, for unions to pick up the cost, or for labor education centers to include child care costs with their class fees and provide the care through regulated agencies.

Conclusion

In spite of the various types of programming available, the labor education structure has not yet been able to provide the necessary tools for women to break through the glass ceiling. Although the importance of education cannot be minimized, developmental learning in a holistic approach that includes women's home, work, and union lifestyles needs to be developed. While meaningful efforts to incorporate women into union leadership are engendered through significant financial and political support within the unions (Trebilcock, 1991), unions and labor education centers need to go further; they must address structural, programmatic, and cultural changes that consider revising union constitutions, rules, and traditional practices and employ new methods of operation, taking into account women's distinct life experience, their dual roles on the job and home, and their own underestimation of their potential. Innovative methods such as credit, CEUs, and Internet programs may attract more women and free women from the burdens of home care by providing child care arrangements. Child care is often the key that may determine women's attendance or absence (Cook, 1992, p.114).

Allowing all opportunities that society can make available will free women to participate fully in educational programs, will add to the numbers of women leaders and active union members, and will aid in strengthening unions in general. When unions join in this holistic approach, there will be no dispute that labor education is a legitimate area of practice within the broader field of adult education.

References

American Federation of Labor and Congress of Industrial Organizations. *Organizing Survey: 1986–87 NLRB Elections.* Washington, D.C.: AFL-CIO, Feb. 1988.

American Federation of Labor and Congress of Industrial Organizations. *Women in the Workplace.* Washington, D.C.: AFL-CIO, 1990.

Baden, N. "Developing an Agenda; Expanding the Role of Women in Unions." *Labor Studies Journal,* 1986, *10* (3), 229–249.

Bierema, L. L. "Development of the Individual Leads to More Productive Workplaces." In R. Rowden (ed.), *Workplace Learning: Debating Five Critical Questions of Theory and Practice.* New Directions for Adult and Continuing Education, no. 72. San Francisco: Jossey-Bass, 1996.

Brickner, D. "Labor Education: Some Questions of Scope and Credibility." *Labor Studies Journal,* 1976, *1* (1), 60–78.

Chaison, G., and Andiappan, P. "An Analysis of the Barriers to Women Becoming Local Union Officers." *Journal of Labor Research,* 1989, *10* (2), 151–163.

Cobble, D. S. "Remaking Unions for the New Majority." In D. S. Cobble (ed.), *Women and Unions.* Ithaca, N.Y.: ILR Press, 1993.

Cook, A., Lorwin, V. R., and Daniels, A. K. *The Most Difficult Revolution: Women and Trade Unions.* Ithaca, N.Y.: Cornell University Press, 1992.

Delaney, J. T., and Lundy, C. M. "Unions, Collective Bargaining and the Diversity Paradox." In E. E. Kosei and S. Q. Lobule (eds.), *Managing Diversity: Human Resource Strategies for Transforming the Workplace.* Cambridge, Mass.: Blackwell, 1997.

Dipoye, R. L. "Problems and Progress of Women in Management." In K. Koziara (ed.), *Working Women: Past, Present, Future*. Industrial Relations Research Series. Washington, D.C.: Bureau of National Affairs, 1987.

Dirkx, J. M. "Human Resource Development as Adult Education: Fostering the Educative Workplace." In R. Rowden (ed.), *Workplace Learning: Debating Five Critical Questions of Theory and Practice*. New Directions for Adult and Continuing Education, no. 72. San Francisco: Jossey-Bass, 1996.

Eaton, S. C. "Women in Trade Union Leadership: How More Women Can Become Leaders of Today's and Tomorrow's Unions." In K. Koriaza (ed.), *Working Women: Past, Present, Future*. Industrial Relations Research Series. Washington, D.C.: Bureau of National Affairs, 1987.

Eaton, S. C. "Women Workers, Unions and Industrial Sectors in North America." In *Equality for Women in Employment; An Interdepartmental Project*. Geneva: International Labour Office, Oct. 1992.

Elkiss, H. "Training Women for Union Office: Breaking the Glass Ceiling." *Labor Studies Journal*, Summer 1994, pp. 25–41.

Glazer, N. Y. *Women's Paid and Unpaid Labor*. Ithaca, N.Y.: Cornell University Press, 1992.

Goldberg, M. J. "Top Officers of Local Unions." *Labor Studies Journal*, Winter 1995, pp. 3–23.

Gray, L. "Labor Studies Credit and Degree Programs: A Growth Sector in Higher Education." *Labor Studies Journal*, 1976, *1* (1), 41.

Gray, L. A. "The Route to the Top: Female Union Leaders and Union Policy." In D. S. Cobble (ed.), *Women and Unions*. Ithaca, N.Y.: ILR Press, 1993.

Institute for Women's Policy Research. "What Do Unions Do for Women." In *Research-in-Brief*. Washington, D.C.: U.S. Department of Labor, Mar. 1994.

Koziara, K. S., and Pierson, D. "Barriers to Women Becoming Union Leaders." In B. D. Dennis (ed.), *IRRA 33rd Annual Proceedings, Special Labor Market Groups*, 1980.

Kruse, D. L., and Schur, L. A. "Gender Differences in Attitudes Toward Unions." *Industrial and Labor Relations Review*, Oct. 1992, pp. 82–102.

Labor Education Program. School of Labor and Industrial Relations. Michigan State University. *Leadership Training Project Survey and Survey Result*. East Lansing: School of Labor and Industrial Relations at Michigan State University, 1991.

Trebilcock, A. "Strategies for Strengthening Women's Participation in Trade Union Leadership." *International Labour Review*, 1991, *130* (4), 407–426.

United Auto Workers. *Women in the UAW*. Detroit: UAW, Apr. 1993.

M. CATHERINE LUNDY is associate professor in the School of Labor and Industrial Relations, Labor Education Program, at Michigan State University, East Lansing, Michigan.

*The authors use personal examples and outline career development
theories in an exploration of diversity issues regarding women's career
development.*

Diversity Issues in Women's
Career Development

Juanita Johnson-Bailey, Elizabeth J. Tisdell

We were in Paris on the banks of the Seine waiting for a tour boat. Libby (my
coauthor of this chapter) spoke French fluently, while I struggled with the language even though I had taken French for several years. The disparity between
my dismal efforts and Libby's ease with words and phrases that I had never been
taught was striking. My teacher had emphasized learning French in case I
(Juanita) was ever lucky enough to dine in a French restaurant. Had her expectations influenced her teaching and my learning? My French teacher, a young
white woman who had lived in Paris and worked as an interpreter at the United
Nations, saw my learning a foreign language within limited parameters. Did she
ever imagine that I would visit Paris? While there are other factors that contributed to my deficient language usage, research suggests that teacher expectation is a major factor in student success (Sadker and Sadker, 1994). Why did
she expect that I would never need or use French outside of a fortunate meal at
a fancy eatery?

Personal Career Stories

Our backgrounds seem similar on paper: Catholic school, terminal degrees from
the same university with adult education majors and women's studies minors,
and jobs in the professorate. Yet our life paths have been different because they
have been shaped by our racial, gendered, and class identities. Writing this
chapter has given us the opportunity to reflect on diversity and socialization in
women's career development with respect to our own life stories.

Juanita's Story. It is impossible to think of career development without
considering my positionality as an African American woman who came of age

in a working-class family in the segregated American South. My background dictated I would work. How else does one survive living on the fringes of a society where employment and existence are precarious? I cannot remember a single African American woman from my childhood who did not work.

These recollections are framed within the equally important context of the gender constraints of being a woman in a patriarchal society. The women of my race and class were bound by the interlocking issue of gendered assignments. We were mostly housekeepers, cooks, and laundresses. And when the working-class and working-poor peripheries were removed, we were mostly nurses and teachers.

Which of my two major positions was more important in determining my eventual work life: race or gender? It is inconceivable that such a question should be posed and equally unimaginable it could be answered. Race was the first constraint of which I was aware. This parallels the nation's history. In the modern era, first came civil rights for blacks, and then the new women's movement started. Yet I personally was cognizant of the lives and circumstances of the women in my mother's circle who spent their lives caring for others.

I believed I would always work, and with an education, I might be a teacher or a nurse. Certainly either of those seemed more a career than the other choices, but it was also a selection from a menu of limited options, since they also were vocations limited by gender and race.

So how did I end up as a college professor at a major research university? I arrived at academia's door via the path of semidirected happenstance that Catherine Bateson describes in *Composing a Life*. The idea of a doctorate had always held great appeal, but it seemed a hopeless dream. I did not know how to pursue it or whom to ask, so I pursued options where I had apparent talent and some encouragement. As the editor of my high school newspaper, I thought I had writing talent, and a journalism professor informed me that his newspaper, part of the Knight-Ridder chain, was looking for young African Americans. His help and advice led to a brief stint for a city daily. Although this was an exciting job, I gave it all up to get married. Failing to heed my editor's advice that I could have both a career and family, I quit and relocated. My boss's message, framed in the context of the early 1970s, did not seem realistic. Later, seeking just a job, I landed in public relations, a field somewhat related to my newspaper background.

Exposure to this working world that was biased against an assertive and vocal young woman led me to a dramatic employment shift and to two decades with federal and state human rights offices, where the women were predominantly the worker bees, field investigators, and the men, mostly attorneys, were leading the way. Even in this area where the focus was on rights, it never occurred to me that I was merely working and not building a future. There was no critical reflection. Seemingly socialized to labor and not to question, working out my ethic of care seemed noble and fulfilling.

After twenty years in the labor force, two women supervisors in my last human rights job said, "You are smart. You are good at training. Get out of this dead-end job. Go to school. Get your doctorate. And this is how we will help you make a way." They apparently perceived I was capable of more, and during a casual conversation I voiced my deferred dream. They understood about the dreams of the disenfranchised, as one was Cuban, the other African American. With these women's help, my career idea was rekindled and I came up with a plan. Finally, I was mentored consistently and directly. Mentoring became more than a casual conversation of, "You might have talent in this area. Have you ever thought of. . . ?"

During my doctoral program, three more mentors stepped forward. The coeditor of this chapter became a supporter and mentor friend by just recognizing that I was isolated—one of only two African American students in the program. This friendship led to collaboration, which led me to two mentors—my dissertation cochairs, an African American woman and a white male—who helped me gain access to an academic career.

Libby's Story. The first time I was asked about my "career development," the question seemed quite odd. The concept sounds like something planned along the lines of Donald Super's stages of career development (discussed in Chapter One of this volume), which does not fit my life experience.

Until 1992 I freely chose my different jobs and public work roles. I basically fell into them as a girl from a white middle-class Irish-Catholic family who was never socialized to plan "a career." Yet there are connecting threads in my career development, and they have been shaped by my gender, race/ethnicity, and class background.

I was born in the late 1950s and grew up in a coastal suburban town just north of Boston that was all white, mostly middle class, and largely Jewish and ethnic Catholic. I was one of five children in a middle-class Irish-Catholic home. Since I was a "good student" in high school, I was enrolled in a college preparatory track as part of class privilege—something that was not true of the girls from working-class families, who lived on "the other side of the tracks." They were routed into the "business classes" that prepared them to be secretaries or cosmetologists. Despite my class privilege emphasizing a college education, as a girl, I was socialized to believe that although I could use my college education to do some sort of paid professional work, I would get married and have children. My for-pay work would be secondary to my husband's career.

Unlike many other girls, I was strongly encouraged by a high school teacher to major in math in college. His actions may have been based on the fact that he and my mother were colleagues. Since my math teacher was someone I liked and admired, I heeded his advice, completing a B.A. in math in 1977.

Although mathematics was fun for me, I found personal meaning in fields that questioned the meaning and purpose of life—religion, spirituality, psychology, sociology, and social work—so I nurtured these interests through involvement with the on-campus Catholic church organization. Shortly before graduation, I was offered a position as a campus minister by a nun who became a significant mentor. I never would have sought such a position because I thought that only priests or nuns could do such work. Nevertheless,

I accepted the job and was well mentored by Sister Marie, who also convinced me to pursue a master's degree in religion. After completing the master's, I worked as a campus minister for the next ten years on two different college campuses and discovered that what I liked most about my jobs were the occasions when I taught adult students.

During those ten years, my feminist consciousness often led to my being at odds with the Catholic church's position on issues related to women and sexuality. I knew I could not work for the church forever. Then my Irish-American priest-boss suggested that if I were to continue teaching in higher education, I should get a doctorate. Although I came from an educated family, I would never have thought of this path. At his suggestion I began gathering information about doctoral programs. Based on my experience teaching adult students and familiarity with the work of Paulo Freire, I discovered adult education as a field of study.

It was not until I was well into my doctoral program that I viewed myself as having a career as a faculty member. I loved teaching but did not know the codes or rules for getting a faculty job. But I had an assistantship, a sort of privileged position that gave me easy access to the faculty. At first I was timid about asking directly, but then I watched male student colleagues seeking help, and so I too began asking. As a result, I was extremely well mentored by two faculty members. Learning the rules helped me intentionally plan a career and eventually enter the professorate. In my opinion, this is one of the secrets of intentional career development: seek out good mentors and ask for help.

The Literature on Diversity Issues in Women's Career Development

Overall the literature on diversity relative to women's career development is extrapolated from studies that have been conducted on middle-class white men. Such studies discount the experiences of women, persons of color, and members of the working class and other socioeconomically disadvantaged groups. This is true of Donald Super's career development theory, which is widely cited and used. His theory discounts how limited exposure to role models, gendered societal expectations, and attempts to balance these two fundamental concerns affect a woman's career development (Gottfredson, 1981; Harmon, 1970; Osipow, 1966). In addition to Super's popular career development theory, Holland (1985) set forth a theory that relies on psychological measures, a Person-Environment Fit Theory, which attempts to match one's abilities and/or interests to job requirements. A major flaw regarding this theory's applicability to women is that it does not consider the limiting effects of socialization. Although ascertaining a person's interests can help determine a suitable career path, what happens when large segments of the population, such as women, and especially women of color, have been encouraged to limit their interests severely? Perhaps career development concepts based on social learning theories hold the greatest significance for women's career development models. Lent, Brown, and Hackett (1996), Krumboltz (1991), and Farmer (1997) have conducted studies using Bandura's social learning theory and have considered how environmental influences, self-efficacy, and sex role expectation can affect career development.

Indeed Farmer and others (1997) seemed a good template for analyzing our career paths and encouraged us to begin with a personal examination of our career journeys. When reviewing our narratives in the light of gender, race, and class aspects, along with the literature on diversity issues in women's career development, we found similarities and differences. First, we will consider issues related to diverse career socialization. Second, we will consider how diverse groups of women deal with external obstacles to their career development. Finally, we will examine mentors' roles.

Career Socialization Issues

Our career paths have been affected by socialization. We envisioned ourselves doing only jobs that we were exposed to. Thus, at every juncture along the way, we chose from a menu of limited options dictated by our gender, class, race, and cultural backgrounds. For both of us, the models of women in professional roles tended to be caretakers—teachers and nurses. The literature is replete with a discussion of the importance of role models in providing examples of career options for women and people of color (Cohn, 1997; Peterson, 1997).

Furthermore, as is the case with most other women, both of us considered work choices with the idea of having children. Our plans for motherhood and our sex role socialization, which dictates that women are responsible for the family, affected our career decisions (Caffarella, 1992; Farmer and Associates, 1997; Gilligan, 1982; Morrison, 1992).

Both of us were socialized as caretakers. Add to this socialization the compounding factor of race, ethnicity, or class, and the ingrained or expected silence that accompanies these issues, and the result is that disenfranchised women are expected to be submissive and passive (Collins, 1991; hooks, 1989; Johnson-Bailey and Cervero, 1997). We learned how to pursue our goals from watching our white and black male peers and colleagues.

But in addition to our similarities, there are distinct differences in our careers. Libby's obstacles to success were few, attributable to being from a white, middle-class, college-educated family; she knew how to negotiate educational systems. But as a woman she did not know how to translate education to professional work. This know-how had been imparted to her brothers, and they were actively and directly mentored into professional careers. Although Juanita's family placed importance on education, by virtue of their race and class, they did not have easy access to formal education, and thus to knowledge of how the systems of "culture of power" in education worked (Delpit, 1995). Juanita had to learn some of those rules outside her own family of origin.

Dealing with External Obstacles

There are three major topics to examine relative to diversity issues in career development: structural inequalities, negative stereotypes, and psychological impediments. First, our world is made up of hierarchies that order society. The primary barriers of race, ethnicity, gender, class, able-bodiedness, and sexual orientation direct our society, giving advantage to those considered the norm and extra privileges to exceptional members of the normed group. Such impenetrable constraints (structured inequalities) give rise to negative stereotypes about minorities and disadvantage them in career development. And directly related to the societal obstructions are the psychological barriers that are developed in response to them. Those who are attempting to live or to build a career in the light of such barricades may face psychological difficulties.

Structured Inequalities. Women are not a monolithic group, yet most of the literature on women's career development presents middle-class, heterosexual, able-bodied white women as representative of all women, and ignores the experiences of women who represent different classes, races, ethnicities, and so forth. Although diversity is usually discussed in terms of black and white, we will address it beyond those experiences as well as beyond our own experiences as a black woman and a white woman.

As a group, women are oppressed, a circumstance that is aggravated by various positionalities. There are commonly held beliefs that "twofers"—women who fill two minority categories—are advantaged by their status. Yet studies overwhelmingly show that affirmative action, giving preferential hiring and promotions to qualified minorities, disproportionally advantages white women by increasing their presence and station (Hacker, 1995; Sokoloff, 1992). Asian American, African American, Latino American, and Native American women earn between eighty-three and ninety-one cents for every dollar earned by white women (Amott and Matthaei, 1996; Hacker, 1995), with African American women leading the group and Native American women at the bottom. These numbers and rankings vary depending on job status and positions but are not significantly affected even when the minority woman has more education and seniority (Sokoloff, 1992). The reality that women of color earn significantly lower wages than white women while maintaining higher unemployment rates, and achieve disproportionally low educational attainment, speaks to the structured inequalities that exist in this society.

Individualistic in nature, American society professes to judge individuals solely on merit. Yet the idea of meritocracy is a myth. American society judges the person or group based on position in the various strata but gives the illusion of worth rather than preference. Members of the dominant group in America, whites, are often unaware of their "invisible knapsack" of privilege (McIntosh, 1989) and how it operates to advantage them in the world at large and in the workplace especially. While systems such as affirmative action that seem to benefit disenfranchised groups are under siege, no one belabors the hidden procedures that benefit the dominant group, such as alumni preferences at universities and colleges and familiarity or relationships with those in the professions or those in power.

In addition to issues of access, the obstacle of the glass ceiling affects the careers of women. Statistics show that once women make it through the door of their chosen professions, they linger at the lower echelons, occupying positions of the workers and lower-level supervisors. But the ceiling still has different meanings for different groups. According to Sokoloff (1992), despite the limitations of the glass ceiling, "glass is breakable: some White women will make it through the broken glass to top positions. Blacks [and other women of color] on the other hand experience a 'Lucite ceiling': Lucite is so strong that while you can see through it, you cannot break it like glass (Henriques, 1991)."

Stereotypical Images of Women of Color. Stereotypes operate at several levels to complicate career development. For most of us they exist at the unconscious level and operate stealthily to inform our actions toward minority group members. For example, if a minority group member breaks an organization's cultural code, the question is often posed implicitly or explicitly, "Is that what we can expect of that person?" Such a question would never be asked of a person who is a member of the dominant privileged group (McIntosh, 1989).

Negative images of minorities also exist as part of the complicity of denying the operation of privilege. If women of color and lower classes are dishonest, lazy, or possess explosive temperaments, then middle-class women of the dominant group are the reverse. This dichotomous thinking privileges one group while disadvantaging another, and it supports the notion of one group's supremacy. As long as stereotypes are part of our thinking and patterns of behavior, meaningful learning and interactions in the workplace are limited.

Psychological Barriers. Several feminists of color have attempted to explain the dynamic way in which the dual nature of gender and race can influence daily life (Anzaldua, 1987; Chow, 1989; Collins, 1991; Hurtado, 1989; Scott, 1991; Wing, 1997). Women of color are affected by circumstances that can make daily psychological well-being a struggle (Moraga and Anzaldua, 1983). Often they are locked out of or asked to choose between groups: "Are you part of the Latina group or part of the women's group?" Such questions can be asked only by those people who belong to or recognize only one group membership, yet "to speak of any one facet more than another dulls the beauty of the whole thing reflecting light" (TwoTrees, 1993, p. 13). Coping with the reality of the interlocking natures of group memberships and dual oppressions and the resulting internalized oppression can be a barrier that restricts the career development of women of color. The idea that life's circumstances hamper one's career seems connected with socialization. Yet it moves beyond the process of socialization when it is viewed in the context of how women of color will directly regard each other within and across racial and ethnic divides. Realistically, women of color can be trapped by stereotypes that relate to their own and to other groups.

One particular trap for Juanita was the idea of African American women being inherently strong. If black women or women of color in general have inordinate amounts of strength and endurance, then why give them help, and why should they expect help or ask for it? Such thinking can complicate job performance and wound the spirit. What is often unseen or perhaps not considered by diverse women is that others are being helped or mentored, invisibly or discreetly.

The Significance of Mentoring

Caffarella (1992) describes mentoring as an "intense caring relationship in which persons with more experience work with less experienced persons to promote both professional and personal development" (p. 38), noting that women may have several different mentors who perform different roles throughout their personal and professional lives. Why would one need different people to address different areas of career development? The answer may be that different mentors are needed because of the diversity of issues in women's career development. Are there special areas or issues that only women can mentor women on or tips that only one woman of color can pass on to another? Certainly. But is this always the case? And what happens when there is no similarly situated person available or willing to do the mentoring? According to the literature, this is often the case. White males mentor more white women and women of color than any other group (Alfred, 1995). This seems logical given that they occupy more positions of power in the professions. In addition, since women are entrenched and invested in the system, such generosity is less of a risk.

Another answer to the issue of who mentors, and why or why not, is centered on the notion of comfort level. Usually people are most comfortable with members of their own groups (Cox, 1993). While this manifests itself as an exclusion of those who are different, it is not intentional exclusion even though the results are the same. Like tends to be attracted to like, so mentoring across cultural lines requires more effort for many people because of the assumed discomfort and unfamiliarity with "others."

Women also report that they mentor themselves by watching others. Libby learned to be assertive by watching her white male colleagues seek guidance and opportunities. Juanita presented at her first conference because her mentor invited her to do so and then stepped her through the process by arranging a series of meetings where she would report on her progress. This was important nurturing since she had never before attended a professional conference. Women often relate that they read journal and magazine articles that provide insight into the cultural codes of their career group.

Implications for Adult Education

What are the implications for adult educators who want to address diversity issues in women's career development? The first step in this process is to realize that most of the literature on career development is about men, and the literature that does exist on women's career development is primarily about white, middle-class women. Adult educators who are teaching classes that deal with career issues should highlight the ways in which race, ethnicity, class background, sexual orientation, marital, or "mother" status affect issues related to women's career development. It is essential to give space for discussion. Too often women's career development literature, especially on diverse groups, is given place but no importance. For example, in an effort to personalize or complete the curriculum, it is discussed the last week of the class or presented to students along with other options as one area to discuss. It is important that instructors combat that piece of the hidden curriculum by giving women's career issues space and importance. In addition, it is important that class discussions and research acknowledge diverse women in nonstereotypical ways rather than present women as a uniform group.

Research and class instruction should include information related specifically to different groups, and the data should not trivialize or treat race (including whiteness as a category), class background, or sexual orientation as an "add on" and therefore "less important." Although not many adult educators teach formal classes on career development, there are ways they can attend to diversity issues that affect women's career options and development.

Another important aspect of attending to diversity issues in women's career development is to address explicitly rules of the "culture of power" (Delpit, 1995) in regard to a particular career—that is, the more one is similar to those in power, the more one is likely to know the rules of the culture of power. Therefore, females, persons of color, and those from a working-class background are less likely to have access to the knowledge of the unspoken rules for career development and advancement (Johnson-Bailey, Tisdell, and Cervero, 1994). Adult educators need to be explicit about the directions for career advancement in a particular field.

Finally, it is clear that more research and literature on diversity issues in women's career development is needed in the field of adult education and in related areas. Writers and researchers in the field need to conduct research about diversity issues in women's career development. It is crucial that adult educators advocate for the value and importance of such research so that the face of career development literature can begin to change.

References

Alfred, M. V. "Outsiders Within: The Professional Development History of Black Tenured Female Faculty in the White Research Academy." Unpublished doctoral dissertation, University of Texas at Austin, 1995.

Amott, T., and Matthaei, J. *Race Gender and Work: A Multi-Cultural Economic History of Women in the United States.* Boston: South End Press, 1996.

Anzaldua, G. *Borderlands: La Frontera.* San Francisco: Spinsters/Aunt Lute, 1987.

Bateson, M. C. *Composing a Life.* New York: Atlantic Monthly Press, 1989.

Caffarella, R. S. *Psychosocial Development of Women: Linkages of Teaching and Leadership in Adult Education.* Information Series, no. 350. Columbus, Ohio: ERIC Clearinghouse on Adult, Career and Vocational Education, 1992.

Chow, E. (ed.). *Making Waves: An Anthology of Writings by and About Asian American Women*. Boston: Beacon Press, 1989.

Cohn, J. "The Effects of Racial and Ethnic Discrimination on the Development of Minority Persons." In H. Farmer and others (eds.), *Diversity and Women's Career Development: From Adolescence to Adulthood*. Thousand Oaks, Calif.: Sage, 1997.

Collins, P. H. *Black Feminist Thought: Knowledge, Consciousness, and the Politics of Empowerment*. New York: Routledge, 1991.

Cox, T. *Cultural Diversity in Organizations: Theory, Research and Practice*. San Francisco: Berrett-Koehler, 1993.

Delpit, L. *Other People's Children: Cultural Conflict in the Classroom*. New York: New Press, 1995.

Farmer, H. "Theoretical Overview: The Longitudinal Study." In H. Farmer and others (eds.), *Diversity and Women's Career Development: From Adolescence to Adulthood*. Thousand Oaks, Calif.: Sage, 1997.

Farmer, H., and others. *Diversity and Women's Career Development: From Adolescence to Adulthood*. Thousand Oaks, Calif.: Sage, 1997.

Gilligan, C. *In a Different Voice: Psychological Theory and Women's Development*. Cambridge, Mass.: Harvard University Press, 1982.

Gottfredson, L. "Circumscription and Compromise: A Developmental Theory of Occupational Aspirations." *Journal of Counseling Psychology*, 1981, *28*, 545–579.

Hacker, A. *Two Nations: Black and White, Separate, Hostile, Unequal*. New York: Ballantine Books, 1995.

Harmon, L. "Anatomy of Career Commitment." *Journal of Counseling Psychology*, 1970, *17*, 77–80.

Henriques, D. B. "Piercing Wall Street's Lucite Ceiling." *New York Times*, Aug. 11, 1991, pp. 1–6.

Holland, J. *Making Vocational Choices: A Theory of Vocational Personalities and Work Environments*. Englewood Cliffs, N.J.: Prentice Hall, 1985.

hooks, b. *Talking Back: Thinking Feminist-Thinking Black*. Boston: South End Press, 1989.

Hurtado, A. "Relating to Privilege: Seduction and Rejection in the Subordination of White Women and Women of Color." *Signs: Journal of Women in Culture and Society*, 1989, *14* (4), 833–855.

Johnson-Bailey, J., and Cervero, R. M. "Negotiating Power Dynamics in Workshops." In J. A. Fleming (ed.), *New Perspectives on Designing and Implementing Effective Workshops*. New Directions for Adult and Continuing Education, no. 76. San Francisco: Jossey-Bass, 1997.

Johnson-Bailey, J., Tisdell, E. J., and Cervero, R. M. "Race, Gender, and the Politics of Professionalization." In E. Hayes and S. J. Colin III (eds.), *Confronting Racism and Sexism*. New Directions for Adult and Continuing Education, no. 61. San Francisco: Jossey-Bass, 1994.

Krumboltz, J. *Career Beliefs Inventory*. Palo Alto, Calif.: Consulting Psychologists Press, 1991.

Lawlor, J. "Executive Exodus." *Working Woman*, 1994, *11*, 39–87.

Lent, R., Brown, S., and Hackett, G. "Career Development from a Social Cognitive Perspective." In D. Brown and others (eds.), *Career Choice and Development*. San Francisco: Jossey-Bass, 1996.

McIntosh, P. "White Privilege: Unpacking the Invisible Knapsack." *Peace and Freedom*, Jul.–Aug. 1989, pp. 10–12.

Moraga, C., and Anzaldua, G. (eds.). *This Bridge Called My Back*. Latham, N.Y.: Women of Color Press, 1983.

Morrison, A. *The New Leaders*. San Francisco: Jossey-Bass, 1992.

Osipow, S. *Theories of Career Development*. Needham Heights, Mass.: Allyn & Bacon, 1966.

Peterson, K. "Success in the Face of Minority Achievement." In H. Farmer and others (eds.), *Diversity and Women's Career Development: From Adolescence to Adulthood*. Thousand Oaks, Calif.: Sage, 1997.

Sadker, M., and Sadker, D. *Failing at Fairness: How America's Schools Cheat Girls*. New York:Macmillan, 1994.

Scott, K. Y. *The Habits of Surviving.* New York: Ballantine Books, 1991.

Sokoloff, N. J. *Black Women and White Women in the Professions: Occupational Segregation by Race and Gender, 1960–1980.* New York: Routledge, 1992.

TwoTrees, K. S. "Mixed Blood, New Voices." In J. James and R. Farmer (eds.), *Spirit, Space and Survival: African American Women in (White) Academe.* New York: Routledge, 1993.

Wing, A. K. (ed.). *Critical Race Feminism.* New York: New York University Press, 1997.

Woo, M. "Letter to ma." In C. Moraga and G. Anzaldua (eds.), *This Bridge Called My Back.* Latham, N.Y.: Women of Color Press, 1983.

JUANITA JOHNSON-BAILEY is assistant professor of adult education and women's studies at the University of Georgia, Athens, Georgia.

ELIZABETH J. TISDELL is assistant professor of adult education at National-Louis University, Chicago, Illinois.

This chapter synthesizes the issues raised in this volume and makes recommendations for organizations, women, and adult educators.

A Synthesis of Women's Career Development Issues

Laura L. Bierema

Women's career development is a complex, diverse process. Women have made advances in U.S. organizations, but the consensus is that they have not scaled career ladders fast or high enough. The workforce is becoming more diverse, and it is in the best interest of the U.S. economy to develop women in their careers. Yet as Fernandez (1999) observes, "Corporate America as a whole, has failed to effectively address the challenges posed by diversity, particularly with regard to racism and sexism" (p. 3).

This volume has raised and explored issues related to women's career development in the United States. It has addressed various aspects of women's career development and identified implications for women, adult educators, human resource developers, and organizations. Women's career patterns have been described, work and family issues have been raised, career development in midlife has been explored, the glass ceiling and part-time arrangements have been assessed, the roles of human resource development (HRD) and mentoring have been revisited, development in trade unions has been investigated, and finally the impact of diversity has been considered.

The Nature of Women's Career Development

The nature of women's career development in the United States is changing, different, and contextual.

Women's Career Development Is Changing. The chapter authors have described how women's career development is changing and how these changes parallel shifts in the U.S. economy and workplace. The workplace is significantly more diverse, as all the chapter authors have pointed out. The changes are driven by the information age, shifts in career life cycles (Schreiber), a slight erosion of structural inequalities (Inman; Johnson-Bailey and Tisdell), and demands for work-life balance (Brumit Kropf; Wentling).

The Information Age. The shift from the industrial to the information age is well underway. For both women and men, it still is not clear what career development means in an information age, where knowledge is doubling every few years and how well you learn is becoming more important to competitiveness. No longer are women competing against male brawn in the workplace. Instead they are competing brain-to-brain. This shift has significantly leveled the playing field when it comes to competing for jobs.

Improved technology has changed how and where work is done. Technology has the potential to break down geographical and social barriers and provide greater flexibility to workers. Many workers are now telecommuting. Women view telecommuting as positive, because it helps them balance family demands more readily. Schreiber identifies the risks of telecommuting as being isolation and segregation into typically female jobs that have little potential for advancement; Inman, however, holds out a more positive view. Although technology holds promise, women should proceed with caution and assess the benefits before adopting technological enhancements such as telecommuting.

Shifts in Career Life Cycles. Shifts in career life cycles are apparent as careers become fluid. Women's careers are characterized by periods of interruption and alternative work arrangements (Schreiber). Many women also work part time and are part of the contingent workforce (Brumit Kropf; Schreiber). The expectation that one will spend a career with the same organization is quickly becoming a thing of the past, and even now is more a novelty than the norm. Today people are much more likely than in the past to change careers and organizations several times, a change fueled by dual career couples and low organizational loyalty in an era of downsizing and reorganizing (Wentling).

Slight Erosion of Structural Inequalities. Despite more equal opportunity, women are still segregated into typically female careers, and the wage gap persists. Women earn seventy-six cents for every dollar men earn (U.S. Bureau of Labor Statistics, 1998), with the average managerial level differential at seventy-four cents. The data worsen based on race. According to one study, for every dollar men earned, African American women earned fifty-eight cents, Hispanic women earned forty-eight cents, and Asian and other women earned sixty-seven cents (Catalyst, 1997). Social expectations of and assumptions about women's roles continue to have an impact on their career opportunities and development, as Johnson-Bailey and Tisdell depict. Although the landscape of career development is changing, problems of discrimination and equal access endure. Inman notes that the glass ceiling is still unbroken. Although there are more women in positions of power in organizations than in the past, progress has been slow. In 1997 there were only 61 female top earners in Fortune 500 companies out of 2,458 top earners. Women were 2.5 percent of the total (Catalyst, 1997).

Demands for Work-Life Balance. Women struggle with work and family balance, regardless of race, class, or career path. For example, they still are expected to be the primary caregivers to children and aging parents, despite the facts that dual earner marriages comprise 42.7 percent of all families and many women balance working with single parenting. Both Wentling and Brumit Kropf detail the conflicts and burdens these social role expectations create for women.

Women's Career Development Is Different. Women's career development cannot be approached with a "one size fits all" mentality. Positionality and interruption and alternative arrangements influence women's career development.

Positionality. Johnson-Bailey and Tisdell point out that career development is affected by social position according to race, gender, sexual orientation, and class. Career development models based on white male experience are inadequate to describe women's patterns of exiting and entering the workforce multiple times, and differences in education, class, and race have a bearing on women's career development prospects and progress.

Interruption and Alternative Arrangements. Women are much more likely than men to have career interruptions, change careers, and work part time. Schreiber's chapter shows how women create different strategies for balancing work and family, and both Wentling and Brumit Kropf describe some of these strategies. Women's career development needs change across the lifespan, as Mott illustrates with the aging population and the choice or need to continue working past the traditional retirement age.

Women's Career Development Is Contextual. Women's career development is not a simply a women's issue. It is a social issue. Patriarchal segregation and discrimination, workforce diversity, and technology characterize the social context.

Patriarchal Segregation and Discrimination. Systemic discrimination is prevalent in a work system designed and controlled by white males. The organizational culture benefits men more readily than women and rewards behavior emulating the prevailing male-dominated leadership. The U.S. government has implemented several measures to equalize the playing field, such as Title VII of the Civil Rights Act, the executive order implementing affirmative action, and the recent passage of the Family and Medical Leave Act. Systemic discrimination runs deep, however, and even institutions aimed at empowerment discriminate, as Lundy points out in the case of trade union leadership access to women.

Workforce Diversity. Workplace diversity is driving change. Both customers and workers are increasingly diverse, and some companies are finding it advantageous to encourage diversity. Organizations may bow to consumer pressure before changing workplace policy and culture of their own volition. Diversity should be included in all strategic business plans, and managers should be held accountable for progress.

Measures Organizations Can Adopt

Organizations need to understand that women's career development is different and recognize that retaining women is a business issue. Women now make up almost 50 percent of the workforce, and the buying power of women in the

U.S. economy is up to 51 percent (Lucas, 1998). Thus, it makes business sense to promote women into positions where they hear customer feedback and make decisions. Progressive organizations are working to attract and retain women. Among the measures that organizations can take are creating infrastructure supportive of women's career progress, developing innovative HRD programs, and supporting work-life balance for all employees.

Creating Infrastructure Supportive of Women's Career Progress. To fulfill their responsibility to promote women's career development, organizations must create infrastructure supportive of women. The organization's culture, structure, policies, and rewards must be consistent with promoting diversity and women in the organization.

Culture. Wentling (1996) argues that organizations must systematically identify barriers and biases in its culture and work to eliminate them. Corporate ranks need to be educated about systemic discrimination and the benefits of diversity. Fernandez (1999) emphasizes that corporate America's failure to deal adequately with diversity is grounded in nonholistic approaches to eliminating race and gender discrimination.

Structure. If organizations are to create infrastructure supportive of women's career development, Fernandez (1999) suggests they have to dismantle bureaucracy. The problems with current organizational structure are that it inhibits innovation, wastes knowledge-based resources, and is inflexible, political, competitive, and homogeneous. Newer models of organizing are now appearing in the literature (see Helgesen, 1990, Wheatley, 1992). Structure is addressed in this volume through McDonald and Hite's call for more structured HRD activities, Hansman's advocacy of formal mentoring programs, Lundy's argument for more holistic development of women labor leaders, and both Wentling and Brumit Kropf's proposals for changing the structure of the work day, pace, and venue.

Policies. Career development processes should be based on bias-free tools and equal access. Organizations must develop policies that promote workplace flexibility such as flextime, job sharing, and other family-friendly policies (Brumit Kropf; Schreiber; Wentling). They need to promote upward mobility of women by making it a strategic objective and build the advancement of a diverse workforce into succession planning. They must also comply with federal and state statutes that seek equal opportunity and access in the workplace.

Rewards. Two factors that hinder women's career development relate specifically to organizational life: bosses who failed to encourage or guide career progression, and discrimination (Wentling, 1996). Managers must be held accountable for supporting women's career development and diminishing discrimination. The old managerial adage that "what gets measured gets done" has great applicability to women's advancement. Organizations should reward managers who promote women's careers. When eroding unequal treatment is tied to performance and compensation, it takes on a higher level of importance by all employees.

Creating Innovative Human Resource Development Programs. Human resource developers play a key role in women's careers. Fernandez (1999) found that the human resources area that employees rate the lowest is career planning, counseling, and development, speculating that this is because companies do not have career development strategies, limited time and awareness exist to address career development issues, neither managers nor employees have received training in career planning, and neither employees nor managers have viewed career development as a shared responsibility. Catalyst (1998b) also identifies having specific career development and advancement paths as important variables for women's success. McDonald and Hite offer several strategies in their chapter for developing women in organizations that have the potential to counter the inadequate development that takes place in many organizations, and Hansman has reexamined mentoring and women's career development.

Daley (1996) found that women and minorities are more dependent on formal, objective factors such as education, prior experience, and performance ratings for career success than are white males, and that the career advice and mentoring that women receive is not linked to social decision-making networks. Thus, women and minorities often lack the organization fit that is important for hiring and promotion. HRD can respond by more aggressively offering developmental programs for women. Steps that organizations can take to develop more effective career planning and counseling services include training both managers and employees on the roles and responsibilities associated with career development; assessing employees' knowledge, skills, and performance; conducting self-analysis to enhance self-understanding; listening to employees' goals and aspirations; assisting employees with establishing realistic goals; committing to specific action plans; assessing the process; and holding managers accountable (Fernandez, 1999). McDonald and Hite offer several approaches to HRD—for instance, single-gender development programs and work with individual employees to create career plans.

Supporting Work-Life Balance for All Employees. The issue of balancing work and family is more than a women's issue. It is a social and organizational issue. Balancing work and family can affect the bottom line positively, as can attention to diversity. Organizations should investigate alternative work arrangements, but ensure that they are developmental, not just a new twist on segregation and exploitation. Organizations also need to reevaluate policies and procedures to check for systemic discrimination and other issues that function as deterrents to women's career development. Ignoring the needs of women is costly.

Strategies Women Can Apply to Advance Their Careers

Organizations have a responsibility to create equitable, accessible work environments, but women also have a responsibility to manage their own career development. Inman is quite adamant on this point in her chapter. Women need to be aware of work context, take responsibility for their career development, and be strategic in their career planning.

Be Aware of Work Context. Awareness is the first step toward meaningful change. Previous studies have shown that women are either unaware or in denial about discrimination in their own career experience (Bierema, 1994; Caffarella, Clark, and Ingram, 1997). Wentling (1996) found that women lack career strategy and political savvy, and that these deficiencies hinder career development. Women need to be aware of discrimination, unequal pay, disparate treatment, sexual harassment, corporate culture, and how to align themselves with mentors and other allies. Women would also benefit by sharing their career stories with each other to establish that they are not alone in the struggles of managing careers.

Take Responsibility for Career Development. Women need to take responsibility for their own career development, particularly as careers are becoming more fluid and contingent workers are increasing in numbers. Most organizations expect employees to manage their own careers, though with organizational support. Women need to chart their course and be assertive about seeking the right mentoring to excel, as Johnson-Bailey and Tisdell suggest.

Be Strategic in Career Planning. Rather than allowing a career to happen haphazardly, women need to create career strategies. They also need to think strategically about how they want to balance work and family, as Brumit Kropf and Wentling describe. Women have proved that they are highly creative at finding ways of balancing life and work and need to continue seeking creative solutions and pushing their organizations for innovative work scheduling and design. Inman suggests that women develop self-awareness, seek multiple mentors, integrate work and family, and develop fluid and customized careers. These are important steps in developing awareness of goals and values in the progression through a career.

Actions That Adult Educators Can Take

Career development is everyone's responsibility. Adult educators are uniquely positioned to educate both organizations and women about career development. They can make women, men, and organizational leaders aware of the challenges of career development. Adult educators understand the role of critical reflection in defining personal experience and social dynamics. They can work with learners to help them become more aware of discrimination, strategies to decrease it, and alternative career opportunities available. It is recommended that adult educators create learning experiences that foster critical reflection and self-exploration in relation to careers, build career development topics into teaching, and work to develop a comprehensive theory of women's career development. Johnson-Bailey and Tisdell also underscore this point.

Foster Critical Reflection and Self-Exploration in Relation to Careers. Adult educators can facilitate the process of self-exploration and critical assessment of the work context.

Self-Exploration. Fernandez (1999) believes that one of the most power-ful forces of change in organizations is for individuals to "know thyself." Inman also stressed this in her chapter. "Knowing thyself" happens through a process of understanding the values, stereotypes, and limitations of one's culture. It is also the practice of empathizing with others and respecting different cultures. Johnson-Bailey and Tisdell addressed the importance of sensitivity to diversity as well. Being in a learning state is important in achieving empathy and less-ening workplace discrimination (Fernandez, 1999). Adult educators are experts at fostering critical reflection among learners. The issue of women's career development can be addressed by targeting lessons toward the questions and issues entwined with career development.

Critical Assessment of the Work Context. Adult educators can help women reflect on their career status. Women have been found to accept without ques-tion their achieving lower career status and income than that of men. Schneer and Reitman (1995) found that of 676 men and women M.B.A.'s graduating between 1975 and 1980, fewer women than men remained in the full-time workforce throughout their careers. For those employed full time, women earned less money and achieved lower levels of management, yet they were not less satisfied with their careers than men were. Adult educators can help women be more critical of their circumstances and encourage them to seek a more equal playing field in their careers. Further, they can work with organi-zational leaders to help them see the systemic affects of discrimination and unequal distribution of power.

Build Career Development Topics into Teaching. Beyond encouraging critical reflection on career status, adult educators can build career develop-ment topics into teaching. Opportunities to address career development through teaching include critically appraising the career literature, assessing the impact of power and culture on careers, and developing awareness.

Critical Appraisal of Career Development Literature. Several chapters in this volume criticize career development theory and literature as being based on white male careers. Further, a critique of women's career development litera-ture is that it is usually based on the experience of white women. Adult edu-cators need to underscore the weaknesses and omissions of this literature when reviewing or discussing career development literature.

Assessing the Impact of Power and Culture on Careers. Careers are riddled with learning to navigate organization culture, politics, and rules. Helping learners understand about negotiating culture and power is critically impor-tant. Often the rules for success in the culture are more accessible to white males and are not shared among diverse groups. Helping learners develop strategies for mitigating culture and power is important for adult educators to consider. Johnson-Bailey and Tisdell offer strategies in their chapter.

Developing Career Awareness. Career education that incorporates both life planning and understanding of the environmental context is important (Farmer and others, 1997). Of course, such planning should begin well before adulthood and continue throughout it. This recommendation also assumes that adult educators are good role models and have an understanding of career development across the lifespan. Topics of importance to career development include creating a plan, receiving the proper career training, finding a mentor, seeking feedback, making mistakes, learning through experience, negotiating salary and promotions, handling discrimination or harassment, changing jobs, mitigating power and culture, and balancing personal life and work. These issues are important to adults, are raised frequently, and present "teachable moments" as far as careers are concerned.

Work to Develop Comprehensive Theory on Women's Career Development. Models of career development that fit both women and a diverse workforce are needed. Applying traditional models that were developed using white middle-class males or females is no longer suitable in this dynamic, diverse economy. Schreiber's chapter summarized the inadequate attempts to explain women's career development based on research of men's careers. She has observed that career development for women is different than it is for men, and it is time that both theory and practice appreciate this distinctiveness. A comprehensive theory of women's career development that accounts for race, gender, and class is needed. Other issues of importance include how personality, sex role socialization, career choice, career experiences, and learning account for career development.

One issue that this volume has not addressed is women who are not privileged to enjoy a career. Such women are wrestling on the margins with welfare reform, systemic discrimination, and limited access to training and job opportunities. Further research can help women, organizations, human resource developers, and adult educators better understand and promote women's career development. The research should also focus on redistributing power through career development rather than reproducing it.

It is important that the work of understanding and advancing women's career development continues. Organizations need to claim responsibility for both developing women and making workplaces conducive to a diverse workforce. Women need to be strategic about their careers and lives and understand the work context. Finally, educators can assist both women and organizations in advancing women's careers. Diligence on these fronts will help crack the glass ceiling and eventually shatter it for women in the workforce of the future.

References

Bierema, L. L. "How Executive Women Develop and Function in Male Dominated Organizational Culture." Unpublished doctoral dissertation, University of Georgia, 1994.

Bierema, L. L. "A Model of Executive Women's Learning and Development." *Adult Education Quarterly,* in press.

Caffarella, R. S., Clark, M. C., and Ingram, P. "Life at the Glass Ceiling: Women in Midlevel Management Positions." In P. Armstrong, N. Miller, and M. Zukas (eds.), *Crossing Borders Breaking Boundaries: Research in the Education of Adults.* Proceedings of the 27th Annual SCUTREA (The Standing Committee on University Teaching and Research in the Education of Adults). London, 1997.

Catalyst. *Women of Color in Corporate Management: A Statistical Picture*. New York: Catalyst, 1997.

Catalyst. *1998 Labor Day Fact Sheet*. New York: Catalyst, 1998a.

Catalyst. *Advancing Women in Business: The Catalyst Guide: Best Practices from the Corporate Leaders*. San Francisco: Jossey-Bass, 1998b.

Daley, D. M. "Paths of Glory and the Glass Ceiling: Differing Patterns of Career Advancement Among Women and Minority Federal Employees." *Public Administration Quarterly*, 1996, *20* (2), 143–162.

Farmer, H. S., and others. *Diversity and Women's Career Development: From Adolescence to Adulthood*. Thousand Oaks, Calif.: Sage, 1997.

Fernandez, J. *Race, Gender and Rhetoric: The True State of Race and Gender Relations in Corporate America*. New York: McGraw-Hill, 1999.

Helgesen, S. *The Female Advantage: Women's Ways of Leadership*. New York: Doubleday, 1990.

Lucas, A. "Putting Women in the Driver's Seat." *Sales and Marketing Management*, 1998, *148* (11), 18.

Schneer, J. A., and Reitman, F. "The Importance of Gender in Mid-Career: A Longitudinal Study of MBA's." *Journal of Organizational Behavior*, 1995, *15* (3), 199–208.

U.S. Bureau of Labor Statistics, 1998.

Wentling, R. M. "A Study of the Career Development and Aspirations of Women in Middle Management." *Human Resource Development Quarterly*, 1996, *7* (3), 253–266.

Wheatley, M. J. *Leadership and the New Science: Learning About Organization from an Orderly Universe*. San Francisco: Berrett-Koehler, 1992.

Laura L. Bierema *is assistant professor in the School of Labor and Industrial Relations, Center for Human Resources Education and Training, Michigan State University, East Lansing, Michigan.*

INDEX

Aburdene, P., 38, 41, 42
Academic labor education centers, 78–79
Access issues, 88–89
Adams, G. A., 16, 18, 22
Adaptation strategies, 35–36, 59–60
Adult education programs: diversity issues and, 90–91; employer-provided resources for, 19–20; labor education in, 76–79, 80; part-time employment and, 43, 46, 50; women's career development initiatives in, 100–102. *See also* Training and training programs
Affirmative action, 88–89, 97
Affluence, quest for, 41–42
African American women: career development of, in personal case example, 83–85; elderly, employment of, 26–27; mentoring of, 66, 68; stereotypes and psychological barriers of, 89–90. *See also* Diversity; Women of color
Age discrimination, 25, 26–27, 28, 29
Aging boom, 25, 27
Albert, S. W., 39, 42
Alfred, M. V., 90, 91
Allen, J., 25, 26, 32
Allies, cultivating, 40
Allshouse, K., 26, 32
Alternative work arrangements, 10–11, 96, 97. *See also* Part-time arrangements; for easing work-family conflict, 18–19, 20; for men and women, 20
Alumni preferences, 88–89
American Association of Retired Persons, 31
American Association of Retired Persons (AARP), 31, 32
AARP WORKS, 31
American Federation of Labor and Congress of Industrial Organizations (AFL-CIO), 74, 78, 80
American Federation of State, County and Municipal Employees (AFSCME), 74
American Medical Association, 17
American Nurses Association (ANA), 74
Amott, T. L., 10, 12, 88, 91
Andiappan, P., 75, 80
Antal, A. B., 59, 61
Anzaldua, G., 89, 91, 92

Apple, M., 28, 32
Ash, R. A., 63, 69
Asian American women, 88. *See also* Diversity; Women of color
Auerbach, J. D., 18, 22
Awareness-building: for gender diversity, 54, 59; for women about work context, 100, 101

Baby boom generation, 25, 27
Baden, N., 74, 80
Badenhoop, M. S., 29, 32
Bahniuk, M. H., 63, 70
Bailyn, L., 15, 20, 21, 22
Balin, J., 68, 70
Bandura, A., 87
Bank Street College and Family Life Studies, 21
Barnett, R., 8, 12
Barriers. *See* Career advancement barriers; Glass ceiling
Baruch, G., 8, 12
Bateson, M. C., 40, 42, 84, 91
Beck, B., 1, 2, 3
Becker, H., 41, 42
Becoming Gentlemen (Guinier, Fine, and Balin), 66
Bee, H. I., 25, 32
Beer, C. T., 56, 61
Belenky, M. F., 30, 32, 56, 61
Bell, C. R., 55, 61
Benefits, employee, 19
Bergmann, B. R., 21, 22
Berheide, C. W., 2, 3
Besl, R., 26, 29, 32
Best friends, 65
Betz, N. E., 5, 6, 7, 9, 12
Bierema, L. L., 3, 54, 55, 56, 58, 61, 76, 80, 100, 102, 103
Block, M., 30, 32
Blunt, A., 64, 69
Body-soul integration, 40
Bond, J. T., 18, 23
Boris, E., 10, 12
Brett, J. M., 20, 23
Brickner, D., 76, 80
Brown, R. D., 30, 32
Brown, S., 87, 92

Brown-bag discussion groups, 56
Brumit Kropf, M., 2, 43, 51, 96, 97, 98, 100
Bureaucracy, 98
Burke, R. J., 55, 61, 63–64, 65, 66, 67, 69, 70

Cafferella, R., 38–39, 40, 42, 54, 57, 61, 64, 69, 87, 90, 91, 100, 102
Canan, M. J., 19, 23
Carden, A. D., 68, 69
Career advancement: factors in, 29, 56, 58; HRD advocacy and, 54, 57–58, 59; organizational initiatives for, 97–99; in part-time arrangements, 48; strategies for, by women, 99–100; training opportunities and, 56. See also Executive positions; Glass ceiling; Leadership; Management promotion
Career advancement barriers, 1–2, 33–34, 99, 102; culture and environment level, 75; at glass ceiling level, 35–36, 51, 54, 75–76; group level, 75; individual level, 75; interpersonal level, 75; for midlife and older women, 26–27; in trade unions, 75–76; women's awareness of, 100. See also Executive positions; Glass ceiling; Leadership; Management promotion
Career anchor, 57
Career assessment, ongoing, 11, 101–102
Career development, women's: adult education and, 100–102; alternative work arrangements and, 10–11, 18–19, 20, 96, 97; career interruptions and, 8–9, 96, 97; contextual nature of, 97; distinctiveness of, 5–7; diverse career patterns and, 9; diversity issues in, 83–91; at the glass ceiling, 35–42; HRD initiatives for, 1–2, 53–61, 99; issues of, synthesis of, 95–102; mentoring for, 39–40, 55, 60, 63–69; in midlife and beyond, 2, 25–32; nature of, 95–97; organizational measures for, 97–99; overview of, 1–3; part-time arrangements and, 43–50; patterns of, 2, 5–11; personal responsibility for, 100; positionality and, 97; strategies for, for women, 99–100; theory for, 102; in trade unions, 2, 3, 73–80; traditional career development models and, 2, 5–6, 9, 44, 57, 85, 86, 102; work-family balance and, 2, 7–8, 15–22
Career development literature, critical appraisal of, 101

Career interruptions, 8–9, 96, 97; part-time arrangements and, 44–45
Career patterns: diverse, 9; psychological well-being and, 9
Career planning, 1; benefits of, 60; concerns about, 60; HRD initiatives for, 57–58, 60, 99; recommendations for, 60, 100; strategic, 100
Career socialization, 87
Career-related mentoring, 64, 65. See also Mentoring; Mentors
Careers: fluid, customized, protean, 40, 57, 96–97; internal, 57
Caretaker socialization, 87
Carrier, S., 17, 24
Catalyst, 35–36, 44–50, 51, 53, 58, 59, 61, 96, 99, 103
Catholic church, 86
Center for Creative Leadership, 35, 37, 39, 40
Centers for Learning in Retirement, 31
Cervero, R. M., 87, 91, 92
Chaison, G., 75, 80
Chandler, C., 67, 68, 69
Chapman, N. J., 17, 18, 19, 20, 23
Child care: cooperative, 40; employer-supported, 20; issues of, 17; for labor education participation, 79
Child care centers, employer, 20
Childbirth, 17
Chow, E., 89, 92
Christensen, K. E., 10, 12, 18, 23
Christensen, P. M., 21, 23
Civil Rights Act, Title VII, 97
Civil rights movement, 84
Clark, M. C., 38–39, 40, 42, 54, 57, 61, 100, 102
Class position, 2, 83–91, 97
Clinchy, B. M., 30, 32, 56, 61
Coates, J., 8, 12
Cobble, D. S., 74, 80
Cohn, J., 87, 92
Collard, S., 63, 69
Collective bargaining, 76
Collegial peers, 64–65
Collins, P. H., 87, 89, 92
Commitment: demonstrating, in part-time arrangements, 49; perception of, and mentoring, 66, 67; perception of, in part-time arrangements, 47
Communication, in part-time arrangements, 48
Communications Workers of American (CWA), 74

Community commitment, 41–42
Community resources, 40
Competing urgencies, 9
Composing a Life (Bateson), 40, 84
Compressed work week, 18
Connelly, J., 10, 11, 12
Conroy, D., 56, 62
Contingent workforce, 2
Continuing education credits, 79
Cook, A., 78, 80
Cook, E. P., 6, 12
Cooperative child care, 40
Corporate culture, 36–38; assessment of, in adult education programs, 101; HRD's role in changing, 54, 59–61; race and class diversity and, 91, 95, 98; training in, 56; women's leadership and, 36–38, 41. *See also* Workplace culture
Corporate instability, 37–38
Counseling and support programs: for midlife and older women, 30; for working mothers, 20
Covenant Investment Management, 36
Cox, T. H., 55, 61, 63, 66, 69, 70, 90, 92
Credits: continuing education, 79; lifelong, toward degree, 79
Creedon, M., 17, 18, 23
Crites, J., 6, 9, 12
Critical appraisal of career development literature, 101
Critical reflection, 100–101
Cross-functional job rotations, 59
Cross-gender mentoring, 63–64, 66–67; collusion in stereotypical roles in, 66; intimacy and sexuality concerns in, 66–67; peer resentment of, 67; public scrutiny of, 67; role model mentoring and, 66
Crouter, A. C., 21, 23
Culture of power, 91, 101. *See also* Corporate culture; Workplace culture
Customized careers, 40

Daley, D. M., 99, 103
Daloz, L., 64, 69
D'Amico, C. D., 15, 16, 23
Daniels, A. K., 80
Darkenwald, G. G., 56, 61
Degrees, lifelong credits toward, 79
Delaney, J. T., 76, 80
Delpit, L., 87, 91, 92
Diamond, E. E., 9, 12
DiBenedetto, B., 7–8, 11, 12
Dipoye, R. L., 75, 81

Dirkx, J. M., 76, 81
Discrimination: awareness-building about, 100, 101; against midlife and older women, 25, 26–27, 28, 29; patriarchal, 97, 99; against women, 1, 6, 8, 54
Diversity, 3; adult education and, 90–91; among older women, 26; awareness-building for, 54, 59, 98; corporate America and, 95; external obstacles related to, 88–89; issues of, in women's career development, 83–91, 97; literature on issues of, in women's career development, 86–87; mentoring and, 66, 67–68, 85–86, 90; psychological barriers related to, 89–90; structured inequalities and, 88–89; workforce, 22, 36, 97
Dobos, J., 63, 70
Dogar, D., 35, 36, 42
Doughtery, T. W., 63, 70
Dreher, G. F., 55, 61, 63, 66, 69, 70
Drucker, P., 37, 42
Dual-income families, 15, 16, 44
Duxbury, L., 7, 11, 12

Eaton, S. C., 76, 77, 81
Economic security, part-time arrangements for, 45
Educational attainment: inequalities of, 1–2; of midlife and older women, 27, 28; rise in women's, 15, 27
Educational resources, employer-provided, 19–20
Elder care: employer support for, 20; responsibilities of, 17
Elderly women, 25, 30. *See also* Midlife women
Eldridge, N. S., 67, 70
Elitism: executive career development and, 41–42; mentoring and, 68; women's career development research and, 102
Elkiss, H., 75, 81
Emlen, A. C., 17, 18, 19, 20, 23
Employee retention: organizational strategy and, 97–98; part-time arrangements for, 46
Employer support: company policies and, 10–11, 18–19, 21–22, 98; competitive advantage of, 22; for easing work-family conflict, 18–20, 21–22; employee benefits and, 19; for midlife and older women, 29; organizational measures for, 97–99; services of, 19–20

Employers, benefits of part-time arrangements for, 46

Empowerment of workers, 76

Entrepreneurial careers, 37, 57

Entrepreneurship, 10, 28, 29, 40

Estes, S. B., 18, 20, 23

Ethnicity, issues of, in women's career development, 83–91

Everyday Revolutionaries: Working Women and the Transformation of American Life (Helgesen), 37

Executive positions: factors in advancement to, 58; gender salary gap in, 35–36, 96. *See also* Career advancement; Career advancement barriers; Glass ceiling; Leadership

Experiential knowledge, 37, 78–79

Experiential learning, 30, 58–59

Face time, 44

Fagenson, E. A., 55, 56, 61, 62, 63, 70

Families and Work Institute, 18

Family and Medical Leave Act (FMLA), 8, 19, 97

Family and sick leave, 18, 19

Family-to-work interference, 7, 18

Family-work issues. *See* Work-family issues

Farber, R. S., 15, 23

Farmer, H., 87, 92, 101, 103

Fassinger, R. E., 7, 12

Feist-Price, S., 66, 70

Felmlee, D. H., 8, 12

Fernandez, J., 95, 98, 99, 101, 103

Fine, M., 68, 70

Fisher, A. B., 30, 32

Fitzgerald, L. F., 5, 6, 7, 9, 12

Fitzsimmons, G., 30, 32

Flexible benefits plans, 19

Flexible scheduling, 10, 18–19. *See also* Alternative work arrangements; Part-time arrangements

Flextime, 18

Ford Foundation, 16, 17, 18, 23

Fortune 500 companies: income gap in, 96; women directors of, 35–36

Fortune 1000 companies, women CEOs of, 35–36

Freire, P., 86

Friedman, D. E., 16–17, 18, 19, 20, 21, 22, 23, 37, 42

Fullerton, H. N., 26, 32

Galinsky, E., 17, 18, 23

Gallos, J. V., 56, 61

Galvin-Schaeters, K., 29, 30, 32

Ganster, D. C., 17, 24

Garofolo, P., 63, 65, 70

Gelfand, D., 30, 32

Gessner, J. C., 21, 24

Gilligan, C., 30, 32, 87, 92

Glass ceiling: adaptation strategies for, 35–36, 59–60; corporate culture and, 36–38, 41, 54; defined, 2; HRD strategies for breaking, 55–61; informal learning and, 58–59; in labor unions, 74–75; prevalence of, 1, 53, 54, 89, 96; race and class and, 89; strategies for breaking, 38–40; women's career development at, 35–42; work-family conflict and, 20, 40. *See also* Career advancement; Career advancement barriers

Glass Ceiling Commission, 2, 3

Glass, J. L., 18, 20, 23

Glazer, N. Y., 79, 81

Gleason, 79

Global competition, 54, 55

Goal setting, 11, 50

Gold, 36

Gold, J. O., 29, 32

Goldberg, M. J., 74, 81

Goldberger, N. R., 30, 32, 56, 61

Gordon, J. R., 55, 57, 61

Gottfredson, L. S., 6, 12, 86, 92

Grant, J., 38, 39, 42

Gray, L. A., 75–76, 78, 81

Greenhaus, J. H., 15, 16, 18, 21, 22, 23

Group mentoring, 55, 65

Guinier, L., 68, 70

Gutek, B. A., 6, 7, 13

Hacker, A., 88, 92

Hackett, G., 87, 92

Haddon, L., 10, 11, 12

Hale, M., 55, 61, 64, 67, 70

Hall, D. T., 11, 12, 57, 61

Hammonds, K. H., 21, 23

Hansman, C. A., 3, 55, 63, 65, 70, 71, 98, 99

Harassment, 1, 67

Harlan, S. L., 2, 3

Harmon, L., 86, 92

Hart, M., 21, 23

Health care, for midlife and older women, 30

Held, V., 42

Helgesen, S., 37, 38, 40, 42, 98, 103

Henderson, C., 26, 31, 32

Henriques, D. B., 89, 92

Higgins, C., 7, 11, 12
High-visibility assignments, 58
Hill, S.E.K., 63, 70
Hite, L. M., 3, 8, 12, 53, 57, 61, 62, 63, 68, 70, 98, 99
Holland, J., 6, 86, 92
Holland's typology model, 6
Home-based work, 10–11, 40. *See also* Telecommuting
Homemaker/childbearer role, 7, 9. *See also* Role conflict; Work-family issues
Homer, 66
Hooks, b., 87, 92
Household labor division, 18, 20–21
How to Stay Employable: A Guide for the Mid-life and Older Worker (AARP), 31
Hudson Institute, 36, 42
Hughes, M. W., 58, 62
Human resource development (HRD): career planning initiatives of, 57–58, 60, 99; creating innovative programs of, 99; informal learning initiatives of, 58–59, 60; and labor education, 76–77; mentoring initiatives of, 55, 60; role of, in women's career development, 53, 54–55, 59–61, 99; strategies of, for women's career development, 2–3, 55–61; training initiatives of, 56–57, 60
Hunt, D. M., 63, 70
Hurtado, A., 89, 92
Huws, U., 11, 12

Identity resolution, 9
Individualism, 88
Informal learning, 30, 37, 39, 40; benefits of, 60; concerns about, 60; HRD initiatives for, 58–59, 60; recommendations for, 60
Information age, 37, 96
Information and referral programs, company-based, 20
Informational peers, 64, 65
Infrastructure, creating supportive, 98
Ingersoll-Dayton, B., 17, 18, 19, 20, 23
Ingram, P., 38–39, 40, 42, 54, 57, 61, 100, 102
Inman, P. L., 2, 35, 42, 96, 99, 100, 101
Institute for Women's Policy Research, 73, 81
Interests, development of, 6–7
Interference, family and work, 7, 18
Internal career, 57
Internet union training programs, 79

Intimacy and sexuality tensions, in cross-gender mentoring, 66–67
Intuition, 39
"Invisible knapsack" of privilege, 88–89
Isabella, L. A., 64–65, 70
Ishio, Y., 1, 2–3
Izraeli, D. N., 59, 61

Jacobson, B., 61
James, J. J., 9, 12
Jarratt, J., 8, 12
Job interviews, strategies for midlife women in, 30
Job rotations, 59
Job security, 37–38
Job sharing, 10, 18
Johansen, M. K., 29, 32
Johnson, A. A., 18, 19, 20, 21, 22, 23
Johnson, W. B., 8, 12
Johnson-Bailey, J., 3, 83–85, 87, 91, 92, 93, 96, 97, 100, 101
Journaling, 39
Judy, R. W., 15, 16, 23

Kale, B. D., 26, 29, 32
Kaye, B., 61
Kelly, R., 9, 12
Kerka, S., 8, 12
King, D. W., 16, 18, 22
King, L. A., 16, 18, 22
Knoke, D., 1, 2–3
Knowledge society, 37, 96
Korte, W. B., 11, 12
Koziara, K. S., 74, 81
Kram, K. E., 54, 55, 58, 61, 62, 64–65, 66–67, 70
Krumboltz, J., 87, 92
Kruse, D. L., 74, 81
Kugelmass, J., 11, 12

Labor contract negotiations, 76, 79
Labor education: HRD and, 76–77; for leadership, 77–78; strategies and initiatives for, 78–79, 80
Labor Education Program (LEP), School of Labor and Industrial Relations, Michigan State University, 77, 81
Labor Review Monthly, 26, 32
Lam, M. N., 56, 61
Larwood, L., 6, 13, 56, 62
Late bloomers, 9
Latimer, S., 56, 62
Latino American women, 88, 89. *See also* Diversity; Women of color

Lawlor, J., 92
Leadership: body-soul integration and, 40; community commitment and, 41–42; multiple mentors for, 39–40; in new organizations, 37, 38–39, 41; self-assessment and, 38–39; in trade unions, 74–76, 77–78; training in, 77–78; women's styles of, 38–40, 41
Leadership Training Project, 77–78
Learning environment, 56–57
Learning focus, 37
Learning sabbaticals, 57
Learning styles, 30
Leave policies, 19, 98
Lee, C., 7, 11, 12
Lee, J., 64, 69
Legislative policies, 8, 31, 97
Lent, R., 87, 92
Lewis, A. E., 55, 56, 62
Life cycle, diverse career patterns and, 9, 96
"Line-of-sight" supervision, 47
Loeb, M., 70
Lorwin, V. R., 80
Lowe, B. F., 18, 20, 21, 24
Loyalty, 46
Lucas, A., 98, 103
"Lucite ceiling," 89
Lundy, M. C., 3, 73, 76, 80, 81, 97
Luttrell, W., 56, 62

Mahaffie, J., 8, 12
Maher, F., 56, 62
Making Work Flexible: Policy to Practice (Catalyst), 47
Management promotion: factors in, 29, 56, 58; training and, 56. *See also* Career advancement; Career advancement barriers; Glass ceiling
Manager support: diversity training for, 59; for family-supportive policies and benefits, 21; reward policies for, 98; for women's career development, 98. *See also* Supervisor support
Marienau, C., 30, 32
Marriage, 7, 8
Marsick, V., 37, 42
Martin, J. R., 42
Matthaei, J. A., 10, 12, 88, 91
Mattis, M., 53, 55, 58, 59, 62
McCauley, C. D., 54, 58, 62
McDonald, K. S., 3, 8, 12, 53, 57, 61, 62, 98, 99

McIntosh, P., 88, 89, 92
McKeen, C. A., 55, 61, 63–64, 65, 66, 67, 69, 70
McKenna, C. S., 63–64, 66, 67, 69
Melamed, T., 7, 13
Mentoring, 2, 3, 63–69; androcentric view of, 66, 68; barriers to, 64, 66; benefits of, 55, 60, 63, 65; concerns and challenges of, 60, 63–64, 66–68; cross-gender, 63–64, 66–67; defining, 64–65; elitism and, 68; formal, 55, 66, 69; group, 55, 65; HRD initiatives of, 55, 60; informal, 55, 66; for leadership positions, 39–40; for midlife and older women, 30; recommendations for, 60; role model, 66, 68; same-gender, 67; types of, 64–65; women of color and, 66, 67–68, 85–86, 90; work-family conflict and, 64, 66, 67
Mentoring circles, 55
Mentors: availability of, 63, 66, 67; career, 64; defined, 64; female, 67; friends and family mentors as, 65; male, 63–64, 66–67; multiple, 39–40, 90; peer, 55, 64–65; in personal case examples, 85–86; psychosocial, 64, 65, 67; for women of color, 90
Meritocracy, myth of, 88–89
Merriam, S., 66, 70
Michael, C., 63, 70
Michigan State University Labor Education Department (LEP), 77, 79, 81
Michigan State Winter School for Women Workers, 77
Middle adulthood, 25
Middle-old, 25
Midlife and older women: career and training patterns of, 29; career development of, 2, 25–32; career development strategies for, 30–31; characteristics of, 25–26; resources available to, 31; workforce participation of, 26–27; workplace challenges and opportunities of, 27–28
Mitchell, W. D., 19, 23
Moraga, C., 89, 92
Morale, part-time arrangements and, 46
Morgan, J., 68, 70
Morrison, A. M., 35, 37, 39, 40, 42, 87, 92
Mott, V. W., 2, 25, 29, 32, 33

Naisbitt, J., 38, 41, 42
Narrative assessments, 39

Narrative research, 41
National Center for Education Statistics, 15, 23, 27, 32
National Education Association (NEA), 74
National Study of the Changing Workforce, 18
Native American women, 88. *See also* Diversity; Women of color
Neal, M. B., 17, 18, 19, 20, 23
Nelson, D. L., 63, 70
Networking, 39, 40
New York Times, 18
Nielsen, S. W., 29, 32
Nieva, V. F., 7, 13
Nilles, J. M., 11, 13
Noe, R. A., 64, 70
Nuclear family, 40

Obsolete skills, 28
Occupational segregation, 2, 53
Odyssey, 66
Ohlott, P. J., 54, 55, 58, 62
Older women. *See* Midlife and older women
Oldest-old, 25
Olson, S. K., 57, 61
Organizations: new forms of, women's leadership and, 37, 38–39, 41, 98; women's career development initiatives of, 97–99. *See also* Human resource development:
Orioli, E. M., 17, 24
Osipow, S., 86, 92
Outsiders, 56–57
Overtime, 44

Packer, A., 8, 12
Palmer, P., 36, 42
Parasuraman, S., 15, 16, 18, 21, 22, 23
Parenting, as human issue, 20. *See also* Work-family issues
Parsons, F., 6, 13
Part-time arrangements, 2, 10; benefits of, for employers, 46; benefits of, for women, 44–46; career challenges in, 46–47; challenges of, 46–47; commitment in, 47, 49; critical responsibilities and, 47; for easing work-family conflict, 18, 19, 43–44, 45–46; for economic security, 45; effective communication in, 48; evolving, 49–50; with full-time workloads, 47; for maintaining career momentum, 45; for maintaining profes-

sional identity, 45; need for, 44; negotiation and development of, 49–50; personal flexibility in, 49; prevalence of, 43, 44; relationships in, 49; for skill development, 45; strategies for successful, 47–50; structured planning of, 48; supervision of, 47, 48; for transition to full-time work, 45; visibility and, 47, 49. *See also* Alternative work arrangements
Patriarchal segregation and discrimination, 97, 99
Peer mentoring, 55, 64–65
Peer resentment, of mentoring relationships, 67
Performance evaluation, in part-time arrangements, 48, 50
Perkins, K., 27, 32
Personal learning webs, 39
Person-environment match and Person-Environment Fit Theory, 6, 86
Peterson, K., 87, 92
Phizacklea, A., 10, 11, 13
Pickering, G. S., 29, 30, 32
Pierson, D., 74, 81
Pipelining, 58
Poole, M. F., 29, 32
Positionality, 97
Powell, G. N., 18, 21, 24
Preferential hiring and promotion, 88
Pregnancy and childbirth, 17
Pringle, J. K., 29, 32
Private-public boundaries, blurring of, 37
Productivity, part-time arrangements and, 46, 48
Professional identity, 45
Psychological barriers, of women of color, 89–90
Psychological well-being, career patterns and, 9
Psychology of Careers, The (Super), 9
Psychosocial mentoring, 64, 65, 67
Public scrutiny, of mentoring relationships, 67
Public-private boundaries, blurring of, 37

Quick, J. D., 63, 70

Raabe, P. H., 21, 24
Race, issues of, in women's career development, 83–91, 97
Ragins,, B. R., 53, 55, 58, 59, 62
Ramey, F. H., 68, 70
Rayman, P., 26, 32

Redmond, S. P., 70
Reinventing the Corporation (Aburdene and Naisbitt), 38
Reitman, F., 8, 11, 13, 45, 51, 101, 103
Relationships, in part-time arrangements, 49
Relocation, 44
Resources: for midlife career development, 31; for work-family integration, 40
Retirement, involuntary, 27
Rewards, 98
Riley, S., 65, 70
Rivers, C., 8, 12
Robinson, S., 11, 12
Rogers, 40
Roland, J. M., 41
Role conflict, 7–8, 16–17, 21; employer support for reduction of, 18–20; prevalence of, 18; sources of, 16–17
Role model mentoring, 66, 68
Role overload, 7
Rosen, O. C., 7, 13
Roskies, E., 17, 24
Rosner, J., 38, 39, 42
Rubin, H., 53, 62
Ruderman, M. N., 54, 55, 58, 62
Ruhm, C. J., 19, 24

Sadker, D., 56, 62, 83, 92
Sadker, M., 56, 62, 83, 92
Sandwich generation, 30
Scandura, T. A., 55, 62
Scharlach, A. E., 17, 18, 20, 21, 24
Schein, E. H., 57, 62
Schneer, J. A., 8, 11, 13, 45, 51, 101, 103
Schneider, E. L., 18, 20, 21, 24
Schreiber, P. J., 2, 5, 13, 96, 97, 98, 102
Schur, L. A., 74, 81
Scott, K. Y., 89, 93
Seasonal work, 10
Self-assessment and self-exploration, 38–39, 100–101
Service Employees International Union (SEIU), 74
Sex-stereotyped occupations, 1, 6, 10, 96; midlife women in, 26–27, 28; race and class and, 26–27, 84, 87
Sexual tensions, in cross-gender mentoring, 66–67
Shapiro, M., 30, 32
Silverstone, R., 10, 11, 12
Single mothers, as sole earners, 15
Single-sex training, 56

Skill development, part-time arrangements for continuing, 45
Snyder, N. M., 53, 62
Social justice philosophy, 76
Social learning theory, 86–87
Socialization process, women's, 5, 6–7, 10; career socialization and, 87; race and class and, 83, 84, 85, 87
Sokoloff, N. J., 88, 89, 93
Special peers, 65
Spokane, A. R., 6, 13
Staines, G. L., 18, 23
Stalker, J., 63, 64, 66, 68, 69, 70
Stereotypical images of women of color, 89
Stereotypical roles, collusion in, in cross-gender mentoring relationships, 66. *See also* Sex-stereotyped occupations
Stitt-Ghodes, W. L., 9, 13
Strategic career planning, 100
Stress: of midlife and older women, 30; of work-family conflict, 17
Stretch assignments, 58
Strong, R., 39, 42
Structured inequalities, 88–89, 96, 97
Super, D., 9, 13, 85, 86
Supervisor support: for family-supportive policies and benefits, 21; for midlife and older women, 30; for part-time arrangements, 47, 48; reward policies for, 98; for women's career development, 98
Supervisory positions, part-time, 47
Support groups, 56, 65
Support mechanisms, for training opportunities, 56
Support services, employer, 19–20
Swanson, J. L., 13

Taeuber, C. M., 25, 32
Tarule, J. M., 30, 32, 56, 61
Tate, E. B., 77
Taylor, K., 30, 32
Teacher expectations, 83
Teague, J. L., 19, 24
Technological skills, 28, 29
Telecommuting, 10–11, 18, 37, 40, 46, 96
Tharenou, P., 8, 13, 56, 62
Thomas, L. T., 17, 24
Time management, 49
Tisdell, E. J., 3, 57, 62, 83, 85–86, 91, 92, 93, 96, 97, 100, 101
Title VII, Civil Rights Act, 97
Tittle, C. K., 7–8, 11, 12

Tiven, M., 18, 23
Townsend, B., 53, 55, 58, 59, 62
Trade unions: barriers to women's leadership in, 75–76; benefits of membership in, to women, 73; erosion of membership in, 73; female-majority, growth of, 73–74; labor education and, 76–80; male-dominated culture in, 74; women's career development in, 2, 3, 73–80; women's interest in, 74; women's issues in, 76; women's leadership in, 74–76, 77–78
Traditional career development models, 2, 5–6, 9, 44, 57, 85, 86, 102
Training and training programs: benefits of, 60; concerns about, 60; environment for, 56–57; for executive women, 56; gender gap in, 2–3; HRD initiatives for, 56–57, 60; for midlife and older women, 27, 28, 29, 30, 31; recommendations for, 60; single-sex, 56, 99. See also Adult education programs; Labor education
Trait-and-factor perspective, 6
Travel, 44
Trebilcock, A., 77, 80, 81
Trocki, K. F., 17, 24
Turban, D. B., 63, 70
Two Trees, K. S., 89, 93
"Twofers," 88

Unions. See Trade unions
United Auto Workers (UAW), 81
United Food and Commercial Workers (UFCW), 74
U.S. Bureau of Labor Statistics, 15, 24, 43, 51, 53, 96, 103
U.S. Bureau of National Affairs, 19–20, 23
U.S. Bureau of the Census, 8–9, 13, 25, 33, 51
U.S. Congress, 24, 31
U.S. Department of Labor, 15, 16, 17, 19, 24, 62
University and College Labor Education Association (UCLEA), 78
University of Illinois, 79
Unspoken rules, 91

Van Velsor, E., 35, 37, 39, 40, 42, 58, 62
Vertz, L. L., 64, 70
Visibility/invisibility: in high-level assignments, 58; in part-time arrangements, 47, 49; in telecommuting, 11

Voluntary part-time arrangements. See Part-time arrangements

Wage and salary differentials, 2, 8, 20, 96; awareness-building about, 101; at executive level, 35–36, 96; for women of color, 96
Walden, P., 42
Waldfogel, J., 17, 24
Watkins, K., 8, 13, 37, 42
Weeks, P., 28, 32
Wentling, R. M., 2, 15, 24, 54, 58, 62, 96, 97, 98, 100, 103
Wheatley, J. J., 98, 103
Whelan, K. S., 55, 57, 61
White, R. P., 35, 37, 39, 40, 42
Whitely, W., 63, 70
Wing, A. K., 89, 93
Wolkowitz, C., 10, 11, 13
Women of color: career development of, in personal case example, 83–85; elderly, employment of, 26–27; external obstacles of, 88–89; mentoring challenges and strategies of, 66, 67–68, 90; psychological barriers of, 89–90; stereotypical images of, 89; wage gap and, 96. See also African American women; Diversity
Women-owned small businesses, 28, 29, 40
Women's career development. See Career development, women's
Women's leadership. See Leadership
Women's movement, 59, 84
Woo, M., 93
Wood, M. M., 56, 62
Work, changing nature of, 2, 11, 37, 57, 95–97
Work-family issues, 2, 7–8, 9, 15–22, 96–97; alternative work arrangements and, 10–11; body-soul integration and, 40; career interruptions and, 8–9, 96, 97; challenges in managing, 18; of child care, 17; of elder care, 17; employer support for, 18–21, 99; interference and, 7, 18; of men and women, 7–8, 20–21; mentoring and, 64, 66, 67; overview of, 7–8, 16; part-time arrangements and, 18, 19, 43–44, 45–46; policies for, 8, 18–19, 21, 22, 98; of pregnancy, 17; role conflict and, 7–8, 16–17, 18, 21; of stress, 17
Workforce 2000 (Hudson Institute), 36

Workforce diversity, 22, 36, 97. *See also* Diversity

Workforce Investment Act, 31

Workforce participation: of midlife and older women, 25, 26–27; of mothers, 15–16, 22; of women, 1, 8–9, 15–16, 22, 73, 97

Working mothers, 15, 16, 43–44. *See also* Role conflict; Work-family issues

Working Women, 35

Workplace culture: assessment of, in adult education programs, 101; change in, 37, 54, 95–97; diversity in, 69, 97, 98; HRD role in changing, 54; mentoring and, 66, 69; midlife and older women in, 27–28; part-time arrangements and, 46, 47; patriarchal, 27–28, 41, 91; work-family balance and, 21. *See also* Corporate culture

Work-to-family interference, 7, 18

Wrench, D., 65, 70

Young, B., 9, 13

Young-old, 25

Back Issue/Subscription Order Form

Copy or detach and send to:
Jossey-Bass Inc., Publishers, 350 Sansome Street, San Francisco CA 94104-1342

Call or fax toll free!
Phone 888-378-2537 6AM-5PM PST; Fax 800-605-2665

Back issues: Please send me the following issues at $23 each.
(Important: please include series initials and issue number, such as ACE78.)

1. ACE _____

_____

_____

$ _____ Total for single issues

$ _____ Shipping charges (for single issues **only;** subscriptions are exempt from shipping charges): Up to $30, add $5^{50} • $30^{01}–$50, add $6^{50} $50^{01}–$75, add $7^{50} • $75^{01}–$100, add $9 • $100^{01}–$150, add $10 Over $150, call for shipping charge.

Subscriptions   Please ❑ start   ❑ renew my subscription to *New Directions for Adult and Continuing Education* for the year 19___ at the following rate:

❑ Individual $57   ❑ Institutional $107
NOTE: Subscriptions are quarterly, and are for the calendar year only. Subscriptions begin with the spring issue of the year indicated above. For shipping outside the U.S., please add $25.

$ _____ Total single issues and subscriptions (CA, IN, NJ, NY and DC residents, add sales tax for single issues. NY and DC residents must include shipping charges when calculating sales tax. NY and Canadian residents only, add sales tax for subscriptions.)

❑ Payment enclosed (U.S. check or money order only)

❑ VISA, MC, AmEx, Discover Card #_____ Exp. date_____

Signature _____ Day phone _____

❑ Bill me (U.S. institutional orders only. Purchase order required.)

Purchase order #_____

Name _____

Address _____

_____

Phone_____ E-mail _____

For more information about Jossey-Bass Publishers, visit our Web site at:
www.josseybass.com   **PRIORITY CODE = ND1**

OTHER TITLES AVAILABLE IN THE NEW DIRECTIONS FOR ADULT AND
CONTINUING EDUCATION SERIES
Susan Imel, Editor-in-Chief

ACE79 The Power and Potential of Collaborative Learning Partnerships, *Iris M. Saltiel, Angela Sgroi, Ralph G. Brockett*

ACE78 Adult Learning and the Internet, *Brad Cahoon*

ACE77 Using Learning to Meet the Challenges of Older Adulthood, *James C. Fisher, Mary Alice Wolf*

ACE76 New Perspectives on Designing and Implementing Effective Workshops, *Jean Anderson Fleming*

ACE75 Assessing Adult Learning in Diverse Settings: Current Issues and Approaches, *Amy D. Rose, Meredyth A. Leahy*

ACE74 Transformative Learning in Action: Insights from Practice, *Patricia Cranton*

ACE73 Creating Practical Knowledge Through Action Research: Posing Problems, Solving Problems, and Improving Daily Practice, *B. Allan Quigley, Gary W. Kuhne*

ACE72 Workplace Learning: Debating Five Critical Questions of Theory and Practice, *Robert W. Rowden*

ACE71 Learning in Groups: Exploring Fundamental Principles, New Uses, and Emerging Opportunities, *Susan Imel*

ACE70 A Community-Based Approach to Literacy Programs: Taking Learners' Lives into Account, *Peggy A. Sissel*

ACE69 What Really Matters in Adult Education Program Planning: Lessons in Negotiating Power and Interests, *Ronald M. Cervero, Arthur L. Wilson*

ACE68 Workplace Learning, *W. Franklin Spikes*

ACE67 Facilitating Distance Education, *Mark H. Rossman, Maxine E. Rossman*

ACE66 Mentoring: New Strategies and Challenges, *Michael W. Galbraith, Norman H. Cohen*

ACE65 Learning Environments for Women's Adult Development: Bridges Toward Change, *Kathleen Taylor, Catherine Marienau*

ACE64 Overcoming Resistance to Self-Direction in Adult Learning, *Roger Hiemstra, Ralph G. Brockett*

ACE63 The Emerging Power of Action Inquiry Technologies, *Ann Brooks, Karen E. Watkins*

ACE62 Experiential Learning: A New Approach, *Lewis Jackson, Rosemary S. Caffarella*

ACE61 Confronting Racism and Sexism, *Elisabeth Hayes, Scipio A. J. Colin III*

ACE60 Current Perspectives on Administration of Adult Education Programs, *Patricia Mulcrone*

ACE59 Applying Cognitive Learning Theory to Adult Learning, *Daniele D. Flannery*

ACE57 An Update on Adult Learning Theory, *Sharan B. Merriam*

ACE54 Confronting Controversies in Challenging Times: A Call for Action, *Michael W. Galbraith, Burton R. Sisco*

ACE49 Mistakes Made and Lessons Learned: Overcoming Obstacles to Successful Program Planning, *Thomas J. Sork*

ACE47 Education Through Community Organizations, *Michael W. Galbraith*

ACE45 Applying Adult Development Strategies, *Mark H. Rossman, Maxine E. Rossman*

ACE44 Fulfilling the Promise of Adult and Continuing Education, *B. Allan Quigley*

ACE43 Effective Teaching Styles, *Elisabeth Hayes*

ACE31 Marketing Continuing Education, *Hal Beder*